HOW

//

My Mother's Dream

I want to dedicate this book to my mother. I was able to dream because she dreamed first.

She had a dream of a child that wouldn't have to go through what she did, she dreamed of a child that was a leader and not a follower, she dreamed of a child that was not like any other. And after she dreamed she went forth and worked hard to make sure that I became that dream; never knowing that her dream would go on to help many others around the world.

It is because of her dream that I've been able to teach so many others how to dream. So many people look up to me and look at me for the answers but who do I look up to? God first and then comes the closest thing around me to him, my mother.

For years my mother sat helping me, modeling me, and taking care of me the best way she could. She taught me the things that have helped me achieve my dreams, she taught me how to fight, she taught me how to sacrifice, she taught me how to forgive.

She gave her years to me and I want to do the same for her.

She is we're I found my strength, she is where I found my leadership, I was her dream, that's why taking care of her is mine.

INTRODUCTION

When I first started writing this book it was 2019 and I was going through one of the worst depression I had ever been in. I didn't like my life, I didn't like myself, I didn't really like being here - on earth.

I remember feeling like the world doesn't get me, the world doesn't love me, why am I here?

I wrote as an outlet, an escape, it was my own sense of therapy - it's just crazy because I didn't know it. 3 years later, I've completed this book and I now know why I write.

It is no longer to escape, no longer to run - it is to tell my story, tell others' stories, and to change lives during the process.

I'm not perfect, none of us are - but if you've picked up this book one thing for sure you're just like me - you're a dreamer.

Let me show you how to walk through this world - and dream.

CONTENT

ONE IN A MILLION

: **a person or thing that is very unusual, special, or admired Thanks** for all the help you've given me. You're one in a million.

I'm guessing you picked this book up because you're just like me, you're a dreamer. You believe in something that others may not believe in just yet. That's okay, you are different – and trust me it's good to be different. Who wants to be like the rest of the world, going in the circle day by day that we call life? I want something more, so I must do something more.

Who wants to be like everybody else, who wants to do what everybody else does. – I don't, and in all honesty, it's dope to know that I'm writing to someone just like me.

Starting this off I want to write something different… something that will change the way you think, something that can relate to you and hopefully compel you to do something more, fight for something more, and become something more! I want to help change your life!

So let me start by saying this; I published my first book at 17. I created my first feature film at 18. I premiered that film in a theater at 19 and it did not just sell out; it oversold. Now I'm running two companies; I am one of the youngest Executive Producers to ever run a Netflix Mini-Series. I have built an empire for me and my family. By the age of 26 I was on Forbes and I believe you're next.

Each and every one of those things started out as a dream. So now that I've just hyped myself up, let me be the first to tell you that I'm not perfect and that all of those accolades sound so amazing but that came with a lot of work, a lot of sleepless nights, a lot of tears, pain, suffering, a lot of sacrifice... all from a boy that just had a small dream; a boy that just wanted to be different.

My name is WriterBoy, my job is to create a world that doesn't exist. I've done that with my films and I've also done it with my life. I went from living in the slums of Washington, DC to becoming a mogul by the age of 24-years-old traveling, filming, and building an empire. This all has happened because I dreamed.

Dreaming is the easy part, It's bringing it to life that will have you on your knees crying, begging, and fighting for more. A lot of times it's not us with the problems nor creating the problems in our life; a lot of times it's the world around us that creates the storms that we see.

Nevertheless, we can't control the world, nor the storm – but we can control ourselves.

Your journey to your dream is going to be hard *(yes I said it, you didn't come here to hear lies)* Fighting for my dreams, racing to live a life of fulfillment as I try to push through this world, may be the hardest thing I've done. But for me - it definitely will be worth it.

HAVING A DREAM

You are a dreamer, so like me, you know there are no rules to being a dreamer. There are rules to obtaining that dream, I want to let you know how to obtain those dreams in the easiest ways possible. Being a dreamer you are already promised trouble. you are already promised problems in life. Why add on to the problems and troubles you're already promised? If someone could tell you don't take that road, that one will have your car breaking down, why would you take it? If someone said to you take this one it's less bumps, less traffic would you take it? Or would you make the decision to go down that road, not knowing what lies ahead of you?

The moment you picked up this book, you've already chosen what you wanted to do, who you wanted to be. You've made the decision to take the faster route, the road with less bumps! Now let's see how well you can hear me, and actually follow this GPS.

I'm going to try writing in a way I would want to read, in a way I would want to understand, and in a way a dreamer like me, like you, who really just wants the answers, would like to be told! So here's your first answer..... No! your first answer is No. No, in the first couple of pages you won't find the huge answer to your huge problem; If you're looking for one already, you're clearly like me *(or how I used to be)* and you're more than impatient! *(lol)* No, this is not easy! This will not be easy, and no, you will not always do what you want to do, but you will do what you have to do to get to where you are going in life. And no, you're not always going to be happy, but I think you will be fulfilled.

So right now, what I need you to do is calm down and take a deep breath. It's more to be a dreamer than having all the answers. You see, because once you solve those problems, another one will come and then another one, and then another one. So instead of giving you the answer to the 2, 3, 4, or 5 questions you may have right now, how about I give you the answers to your entire test? Being a dreamer is one thing.

Getting that dream to come to life in the real world is an entirely different moment, a different experience and getting to where you want in life. I realized you don't have to be perfect. You don't have to know all the answers; you just have to fight, and you have to be ready to be that 1 in a Million.

1 IN A MILLION

A lot of people say that chasing your dream is a 1 in a Million chance, and it is. But what they forget to tell you is that you get to choose if you're that 1 in a Million.

If you're willing to work harder than everybody else, if you're willing to sleep less than everybody else, if you're willing to fight harder than everyone else, then you get to choose if you are that one in a Million.

I look at having a dream like a big desert. Picture yourself there - it's huge, it's empty, it's deserted; winds blowing, dust in the air, you find yourself staring into the sun.

Now next to you stands a long line of hundreds of thousands of people shoulder to shoulder on both sides of you - all looking at the end of the desert, all preparing to run. An alarm goes off and suddenly everyone begins running. A small barrier pulls up from the ground out of nowhere tripping everyone up and you and everyone else fall face first to the ground; when you start to stand up you start looking around to see the person next to you get up, turn around, and begin to walk off - walking away from the dream that they so desperately desired.

You however, shaking it off, continue running. Out of breath and fighting for air you begin to see others passing out, getting up, and turning around once again walking away from their dreams, their destiny, their future - just like the one before.

Imagine 4 years go by - Now those hundreds of thousands of people that started chasing that dream the same time as you - are now narrowed down to 3 maybe 4 people; out of thousands. - It's been 4 years of running, fighting, and beating your chest - you're so close but so tired. As you blink slowly, you begin to hear the sounds of the person to your left as they groan from starvation and begin to turn around as you continue crawling towards your dream.

Right as you lay in front of the long awaited goal, a wall suddenly structures in from the ground and the excitement on your face is wiped away.

As you lay shocked the last man beside you gets up from crawling and begins crying as he walks away. What do you do, you ask? You begin to climb that wall! Tired, hungry, sad, hurt, and wanting to give up; the same emotions that everyone else had you continue to climb that wall. you then fall; finally grabbing the light.

You will be that dreamer that gets their dream, but in order to do that you just have to make it to that wall, and climb over it – by any means necessary. You cannot quit, giving up should never be an option.

It's like a video game! You can play that game over 20 times and continue to lose, one battle after the next! But the trick to it all is to never stop playing the game! If you get out of the game now, you get off as a loser. You lost, but if you stay in the game who knows? But if you stay on the course and you just continue to fight until you win; even if you've lost a million times, eventually you will win, and when you do, you can put down that controller as a winner. It doesn't matter how many times you've lost; all that matters is that you just won! Period.

I want to make something clear! Life will be hard, there will always be trials and tribulations whether you're fighting for your dreams or not. I'm either going to work hard for someone else's job, establishment, and life - or I'm going to work hard on what I want to be, who I want to be in life.

You can't escape life; we can't escape life - so how about we at least make our time on this Earth worth it? Before I get started, there's a couple of things that I know you're going to need moving forward and you should probably go get those things. You can get this stuff from anywhere, even the Dollar Tree - you may spend five or ten dollars but …. I promise you that these things are what I used to change my life – and hopefully, if you're able to follow me they're about to change yours too. You're going to need them.

BY THE WAY

I know this book looks thick – trust me I know. Even this is part of the process. Let's do it together.

"Why Should I Read This Book?"

If this is really a question, please reevaluate what you want to do and who you want to be in life and then revisit this conversation with me.

I'm a dreamer – that helps other dreamers not only dream but bring their dreams to life. I believe that everyone can obtain their dream in life, you just have to fight for it.

Now I know some people are like wait Brandon, not everyone cannot get their dream! that's not how life works."– You're wrong.

Everyone can get their dream – life is not set up for only one person to obtain their dream as everyone fails and loses behind them. Yes that's what happens, but no that's not how it has to be, that's just what it's destined to be – The person that made it to the end of that desert wasn't any more special then the guy that turned around at the beginning of the race.

They just did things and pushed through things the others were not willing to do.

Sometimes, once people start their journey and must begin pushing and fighting for their dream, a lot of people realize it's not actually what they wanted.

It's too much time, too much pressure, too much money, too much hurt, too much pain, not enough sleep. – That's when you begin to see people fall off – people fall down – and you begin to see people turn around and give up on their dream - because it was too much.

It's not that they can't get their dream, or that YOU can't get your dream - it's just sometimes it's too much for one person to bear and me out of all people - I understand.

I will never give up, but I can truly understand why people do, I'll tell you more about that later.

"Well Writer, what about a girl that dreams of being the next Beyoncé but can't sing for nothing? What do you say about that?" To that, I say

1. You can only be the new version of you. No one can ever be someone else.

2. That girl that has that dream if she's willing too she can; vocal lessons cost how much? What about hiring choreographers, dance lessons, instrument lessons?

Would it be hard, yes – but could the young woman work as hard as she could to perfect her craft, learn how to be the person she dreams of being, yes she can.

Can she take marketing classes to learn how to get her music out there, invest in herself to get the funds needed to place her music out there, PR, Radio, Television, and even paying to get into events and rub shoulders with the people she needs to rub shoulders with; yes of course. – it would just take a lot of work – and a lot of learning new things, and even sometimes unlearning old things. But she can do it.

Be ready to do all of this for yourself.

If you want something different to happen in your life you must do something different with your life. If you don't want to grow or evolve in life and change your world that's fine – put this book down – and go keep doing what you've been doing. – But if you do want something to change, to become something more, to be something more - bet! Keep reading. I'll help you do that.

Everyone can dream – it takes an amazing, crazy, strong, smart, skilled, and out of this world type of person to make their dreams come true. And I believe that's you.

"Well you don't know me, you're literally just writing a book right now!" I'm guessing you're saying that in your head and if you are - you're right I don't know you – but let me tell you what I do know – I know that for some reason by some way – you got this book into your hands.

You then understood what it was about, and because of something or maybe even someone you decided to open this book up and read …. You decided to figure out what this was all about.

That tells me that you want to know – you want to know if you can win, you want to know if you can really obtain your dream. It tells me you're willing to read to find that out and lol that tells me all I need to know about you. – that tells me that you're willing to learn how to obtain your dream, and that's more than that girl that can't sing pretending to be Beyoncé.

While she's faking her reality you're in rehearsals, Vocal lessons, while she's just hoping on stage and dancing, you're actually in rehearsals -

fighting. pushing, trying to become the person you want to become in life.

Your time shall come, and when it comes - you'll shine.

THE DREAM WALL

So one of the biggest things I've done that helped me begin to curate my goals, see what I needed to do, and then allow me to do it was my Dream Wall. What you do in this world is very simple, very easy! You write your goals on a sticky note – place these sticky notes on your wall, and snatch it down the moment you complete that goal!

There are key points in all of this! First you must place long-term, short-term, and goals of even today and tomorrow on that wall! What you need to get done this month, this week, this year! Put all of your goals on that wall that needs to get done.

Why because you need to be able to see your goals completed brick by brick, you won't see the entire thing but you can see the pieces of your life moving forward. You placing down one goal at a time, no matter how small or how tall, shows you that you're not just sitting around doing nothing - you're completing something; you're pushing forward.

You're doing it. Even if it's just one sticky note taken off that wall - you're that much closer to the bigger dreams, the bigger goals, the bigger picture.

Don't know where to start? Start with the big goal and the big dream that you have and write that down on a sticky note right now - let's place that on your wall. – Now I want you to start to think about all the things it'll take for you to get to that goal!

You see because dreaming isn't going to get you to achieve your dream – so what is? What do you need to do, obtain, build, grow, or learn in order to get into that door, into that room, into that vision, that body, that person, that life that you see in front of you?

You know the things you need to do? You got them in your head? Good now, write them down. One sticky note at a time.

Begin writing the steps and goals it's going to take to get you to point A and point B in your life. Things that you need to do now and tomorrow – after that begin writing even your daily goals for yourself, your dream, your life. You must have balance in it.

Taking the notes off of the wall is very vital as well! It helps you not only feel that you are getting that much closer to your dream but it also shows you that you are moving forward in life. Sometimes this world makes us feel like we are standing still – that you're not moving or improving but you are. - and you need to see that.

You must take your goals down, goals are not meant to last forever – they are meant to be achieved, taken down, thrown away, because you've already accomplished them and you have more dreams, more goals to put up, they will soon be replaced. So - Take it down! – I promise you there are many more goals to come.

I've seen people try my method without actually doing what I've asked and it usually doesn't work for them. Why, because day after day they stare at a wall that has all of these goals on them and sometimes that can become not only overwhelming but can consume you.

It's okay to put goals up on your wall – everyday if you have to, but don't force it. Know what you have to do! Do it! And then rip it off the wall and throw it away.

I write huge things as far as meetings, schedules, calls and more, but then I also do the small things like getting my haircut, finding a location for my shoot, or even buying my mother groceries. I Write Everyday goals for my everyday life as I continue to fight for everything I want.

I promise you this helps! It's better than a calendar on your phone or a note in your notepad app - sometimes you have to write things down, tear things up, and watch yourself achieving the goals around you. This also helps because every day waking up you get to see your future all over the walls – you get to see physically what you see in your head.

I think it is very powerful to wake up every morning and go to bed every night watching your dreams and goals lay on your wall. P.S just make sure you start achieving some of them right away.

//

EXCUSES

ex·cuse

🔊 *verb*
3rd person present: **excuses**
/ik'skyōoz/

1. attempt to lessen the blame attaching to (a fault or offense); seek to defend or justify.
   "he did nothing to hide or excuse Jacob's cruelty"

   Similar: justify   defend   make excuses for   make a case for ⌄

2. release (someone) from a duty or requirement.
   "it will not be possible to **excuse** you **from** jury duty"

   Similar: let off   release   relieve   exempt   spare   absolve   free ⌄

🔊 *noun*
plural noun: **excuses**
/ik'skyōos/

1. a reason or explanation put forward to defend or justify a fault or offense.
   "there can be no possible **excuse for** any further delay"

   Similar: justification   defense   reason   explanation ⌄

I DON'T HAVE THE TIME

I don't have the time.

I laugh as I type this because this excuse has come from so many people from so many different walks of life. – you are not different nor unique in this area! No one seems to have the time.

From my youngest cousin that wants to be a YouTube star to an older friend of mine that wants to be the same thing. Both say they have a lot of things going on in life, not a lot of time, too much work to do – but they're trying. The cousin is in Elementary school …. so there's that and the friend well …… he has a 9 to 5 that he hates but spends most of his time doing than something he loves, so there's that too.

Now I'm not saying quit school nor am I saying quit your 9 to 5 especially if you have bills and responsibilities to take care of – BUT what I will say is this: There are 24 hours in a day – use your time wisely.

What you water will grow. What that means is that if you water your dreams, if you water your ambition; putting in the effort, the work, anything and everything towards building and getting to what is promised to you.

I promise the more you water the more it shall grow. – But if you've already made up your mind that not even 30 minutes to an hour can go into you fighting for your dream then you've already lost the battle. – I don't want you to lose.

Take one of those sticky notes and write on your wall a time frame for the next 6 days that you will specifically leave for yourself and your dreams. Take that time out of the day and just create for yourself, build for yourself, just water your plant.

I NEED TO SLEEP

So there's this huge debate about why you should sleep and that it is better for your body and how doctors say this and how people say that, LISTEN!

How about we hear from those that we are trying to obtain from, people who have gotten to where we're trying to go? For me it was the Will Smith's, the Tyler Perry's, the Spike Lee's of my generation and although these men had different routes, took different avenues to get to where they were going in life they all had one thing in common to me – fight.

Ray J is one of those men in the world that I can say fights for everything he wants in his life – that doesn't mean he's perfect, it means he's fighting for something more for himself and his family. One day, me and Ray were in the studio and he said,

"You know why I don't sleep?"
I asked him why; he replied
"Because the people at the top are not sleeping – and if I sleep and they're still not sleeping – how am I ever gonna catch up?"
I laughed and he continued to say

"They gotta sleep at some point, so if I keep working and then they just so happen to fall asleep for two maybe three hours– I'm that much closer to getting to where they are."

People will tell you not to stay up and work on your dreams – I'm not those people. I'm here to tell you to drink some coffee, take a herbal energy drink, drink some tea. From doctors, lawyers, to police officers they all stay up for their jobs and what they have to do in life.

You're a dreamer and it is your job to make your dreams come true – so if it takes a steak out or two. If it takes pulling double shifts or working over time you should do what you have to do to get to where you are destined to be!

Flip side – now I had to come back and write this in because I want to be very clear on what I am telling you to do – I am not telling you to stay up for an entire week with no drop of sleep whatsoever, do any drugs, or obtain or try your hardest to get sleep deprivation!

What I am saying however is that it's time for you to fight! – As you're sleeping right now I'm up writing the second book that I'm going to be publishing in my lifetime and I'm only 24 (at the time) I'll be 25 in 3 days.

Am I tired?

- Yes.

Do I want to sleep?

- Yes.

Will I be going to sleep?

- No.

Because I have a bus to catch at 8am to New York to meet with one of my friends over at Atlantic Records and it's already 6:18am. I'm telling you that while you're sleeping there's plenty of men and women around the world like me – up working.

Don't kill yourself trying to get to where you're going in life – but at the same time don't sit back and relax thinking somethings just going to fall in your lap – because it's not.

I'M BROKE

Aren't we all? A lot of dreamers have this dilemma – why because we are not who we dream we are just yet and that's okay – it's called our future for a reason it's because it's in our future so understand this:

"It's not about what you don't have, it's about what you do with what you do have."

Before shooting Commercials for Burger King, before writing for Google and Writing and Executive Producing for Netflix, I had one small blue camera my mother had bought me for Christmas.

Before having rigs and gibs I had a tripod that I made myself and younger cousins hold onto like a dolly or a slider, trying to get our shots as smooth as possible so it would look like the movies I had seen on TV.

I started my first company before even hitting 16 and I started it with $0 in my bank account – all I had was some skills and a dream. – You don't need all the money in the world to make your dreams come true.

"But what about this, but what about that"

There will always be a what if, a but this, or a but that – how about you do both of us a favor and figure it out! Just simply figure it out! – No one is going to come and figure this out for you!

So stop waiting for someone to come and whisk you away because it's not happening. You don't have the money and you need it right? – go get it!

Go find a way! Find a how! – and if you can't figure out how - do it with what you do have.

If you can do that, you can do anything. This is what separates the dreamers that will bring their dreams into reality vs. those that will just stay asleep and continue to dream.

I'm not asking you to be perfect. I'm not asking you to even be right – I'm asking you to figure it out.

When I was 16 I began shooting Music Videos for my cousins, artists around the way, and anyone and everyone that would pay me to do so.

I began designing websites for everyone I knew until businesses started hitting me up, I created banners, flyers, mock-ups. I did it all in order to pay for my first book to be published, my first film to be created, whatever I needed to bring my dreams to life.

I was a teen that knew what he wanted and was willing to do anything and everything to get it done. There was no hand out, there was no freedom, there was work, fight, and a whole lot of learning that I needed to do in order to achieve my dreams, accomplish my goals, and become the man you see today.

Money didn't make me who I am – it was my fight that made me who I am, my drive, my passion, my God that made me the guy that I am today. – I say all of this to say – money is not going to get you your future – it is YOU that will get YOU - your future.

Just be patient, fight, wait it out, and if you can't do any of the above please by all means figure it out! Make something work, make it happen. It's easy to say you can't – anybody can say they can't.

It's harder to say I can.

It's harder to say I will.

It's harder to say I'll figure it out.

and then go and Figure it out. - You got this.

Sometimes when you don't have money you tend to not eat & in return you're hungry. So many people are so busy fighting to eat in this world that they don't even realize it's not the money that they're trying to obtain, it's the hunger they're trying to subdue.

Today we wrapped up another production and it was amazing - After we all went out to eat. In this restaurant I sit here looking around as I smile at a all of these other dreamers around me. I realized that we may all be fighting for different dreams but one thing we all had in common, is that we are all hungry (Mentally and Literally lol)

We all want something out of life, we all want the dream, the passion, the escape, but more than anything else, we want more!

That hunger that the people around me have is the same hunger that I have; Surround yourself with people that have the same appetite you have, the same hunger you have, and the same drive that you have, the same passion you need!

Everyone doesn't have to eat the same meal, they just have to be as hungry for more as you are.

In other words, as I sit here I'm surrounded by Directors, Actors, Models, Doctors, Lawyers, Financial Assistants and so many more futures; It doesn't mean that everyone has to have the same dream, they just all have the same hunger.

One of my friends name is Irving Lambert, he's an amazing actor, director, and now model (Lol). But before all of that, before LA, he was my friend, with a dream. I'm not going to give you guys our whole backstory but just know just like me we both came from nothing.

When I talked to Irving from Vader's phone telling me that he was moving to LA I remember asking him what are you going to do there, where are you going to stay, what's your plan?

When I tell you he had the same answer for every one of my questions,

"I don't know."

My friend had packed his bags, filled his car up, and decided to just go and chase his dreams. Now I'm not telling you to pack your bags and leave everything behind but I am telling you that's what he did, that's what Tyler Perry did, that's what Eddie Griffin did.

THAT'S NOT WHAT WRITERBOY DID! But It's what Irving Lambert did and what that sewed in me was strength, fearlessness; seeing him take this huge leap of faith, when all of us had nothing was amazing.

I was scared back then to leave - and look at this guy, ready to jump with no fear of falling. I saw Irv jump, then I saw Vader jump, it was like both of them looked at me and said

"Come on Writer" So I jumped too; best decision I could have ever made.

Irving was not stupid nor foolish he knew it would be hard, he knew it would be a lot, he knew he didn't know all the answers, he also knew he didn't need all of the answer. - He walked by faith, not by sight. He knew he needed to move. - So he jumped.

He's now an amazing and successful young writer, director, and the producer of the Netflix Series "Netflix Dreams"

He would say it was worth it.

I know that finding friends that match you may not always be the easiest thing to do but let me tell you where to start.

When you begin doing the things that you love, moving into areas that you want in life. You will stumble upon people that love what you love, and I promise you that they're searching for people just like you too. None of us want to truly believe we are the only ones dreaming! So go to that model call, that acting class, that next audition, the school for technology, the school for fine arts, go for that internship, go for that moment in time that may change your life because that friend that loves the same thing you love is there - and they're waiting to meet you. Eventbrite might be a good place to start.

//

SOLUTIONS

 so·lu·tion

/səˈlooSH(ə)n/

noun

plural noun: **solutions**

1. a means of solving a problem or dealing with a difficult situation.
   "there are no easy solutions to financial and marital problems"

2. a liquid mixture in which the minor component (the solute) is uniformly distributed within the major component (the solvent).
   "a solution of ammonia in water"

Similar: (mixture) (mix) (blend) (compound) (suspension) (tincture) (infusion) (⌄)

If you are going to look at all of the problems in your life as a sense sable human being, you must also look for the solutions.

So many of us sit in our sorrows, sit in our worries, and all of the problems that come with our life instead of getting up and finding out how to send all of this pain down the drain, how to get over the sorrow, how to get through the mud.

Sometimes you're so comfortable in it – that you don't want to leave it. – But it's time, it's time for the sorrow and pain to be drained, it's time for you to get up. It's time for you to find your solutions.

There are so many people around me that want to do what I do; that want to become the man that I've become and who I'm still becoming - but they aren't willing to sacrifice how I've sacrificed!

You want your dream? Do the work! - Sacrifice.

Even if that means giving up the comfortability of sitting in your pain and sorrow, even if it means giving up all the pain you know and have grown up with. Even if that means giving up your hurt.

Find the solution to your problems.

Whether it's you forgiving a person, figuring out a situation and or path for your future; sometimes your solution could be taking a break and coming back to that project, that board, or maybe even that part of your life.

ANYBODY CAN FIND THE PROBLEM! ANYBODY! I can pick 5 people on the corner of the street I'm walking down right now and tell them my entire life's story and then ask them to help me find the problems in my life.

They'll be able to point out each flaw, each mistake, each transgression - it's a bad decision, it's a horrible mistake, why? Because it's in PLANE SIGHT! It doesn't take a scientist to find the problems within your life. However, it takes a very smart individual to find the solutions to their problem especially when those solutions come from within themselves.

I don't want you to look back at this moment in life five years from now and say

"Okay now it's time for me to let go- now it's time for me to move forward"

Why wait five years to do what you can do now, which is find your solution, make your change, and solve your problem.

I'm a person that believes no matter what situation I've gotten myself into, what altercation, misunderstanding, or miscommunication I may have, it's always something I could have done better.

Even if they've done me wrong, hurt me, broke me - I always look at every situation like:

Yes, they did that, and I cannot control them - but what could I have done better? How could I have made sure I didn't go through this; How do I make sure I don't go through this again?

I like this concept because it keeps me growing. Even if it wasn't my fault or I did nothing wrong - it's still; What could I have done better?

How could I have avoided being in this situation at all?

It's: What should I have done more? What should I have done less? How do I make sure this mistake never happens again?

WHAT HAPPENED IN YOUR LIFE

Okay let me start by saying what you don't want to hear "I understand." I know when we as humans have gone through things in our life at times we truly don't want to hear the words I understand - Why? Because you don't - Do you?

Like do you truly believe the pain I am going through. Do you, right now, truly feel the same way I feel right now? - You don't! So no I don't want to hear you say "I understand."

So let's scratch that out. I don't understand you - I HEAR YOU,

I BELIEVE YOU,

and YOU ARE NOT ALONE.

Everyone goes through different things in life and what might hurt one, would never hurt the other. For example:
One of my friend's mopes around a lot. He's very emotional and at times can be more than your bargaining for - he at times is extremely aggressive and yet loving and caring as well.
He hurts because he feels as if the world doesn't see him, doesn't love him, and he doesn't really have "true friends" around him. His pain is him

feeling like he never fit in, his pain is him feeling like he's never been accepted, His pain is him feeling like he doesn't know where to go from here. - This was his pain.

On the other hand I have another friend, his name is Elisha Anderson; many of you may know him as the amazing talented singer that as an artist blows your heart away, and as a person's smile brightens up the room, loving, caring, and would give the shirt off his back to you.

Elisha's mother died in 2018, he lost her soul, him and his relationship with God had taken a toll. I saw the lifelessness in his eyes for almost two years straight. - This was his pain.

If you looked at both you would think that the first friend suffered the tragic death of his mother by the way he is perceived by the world, by the way he carries his pain and hurt on his shoulders, by the way he has no sense of hope in his eyes.

While the one that has been through that tragedy stands tall, smiles, and has one of the closest relationships with God on this earth that I've ever seen.

I say all this not to say oh your life can be worse, or that someone's going through something more than you - I'm saying this to say that everyone is going through pain,

Whether it's big or small, our pain is our pain. We all handle things differently. We must learn to accept that, take that in, and not belittle one another's pain because just as physical abuse can damage us, so can mental.

When you understand that pain is pain the next step is where do we go from here? How do we heal from here?

Do we hurt others because we've been hurt? Do we throw stones because people have thrown stones at us? Do we confront the world because we feel like it's done us wrong? Or do we damage those around us so they won't damage us first?
What do we do?
The answer to this question? I got you.

First we are not going to become those things that we hate. I think that's stupid, unproductive, and it is just not what we want at all.

Why become something or someone we dislike.
I've seen family members despise their parents and then become just like

them, friends and family despise what they call their enemies and then turn around and act just like them. Why? How does that make sense to you?

The next thing we must do is easy, we must -

BE HONEST

Now first let me be honest with you!

We cannot stop the pain - that's impossible. We cannot erase the past, that's implausible and as far as the future we cannot block the battles and hills that are to come before us. But what we can do is a few things to keep ourselves through this rough process we call life.

The biggest thing I'm recently learning as I watch myself and the world around me is simple. We can be honest with ourselves and we can be honest with the world.

Sometimes it's really hard for me to have those hard conversations with others. Now of course I am an amazing honest guy - but the honesty that I speak of, honesty that sometimes may hurt a person, honesty that could cause friction or discord, honesty that could do all of those things ... but could also bring you and the world around you a lot of peace.

Honesty brings awareness to the world, it brings understanding to others, honesty can bring distance where it is needed, and boundaries where there aren't any.

So yeah there's something that can be feared from honesty, things that can be lost with honesty, but there is also so much more to be gained when you are honest - even when it's hard to be.

So I say - tell the truth, tell the person or people how you feel, not everyone, not those around them, but that person. And like my best-friend Samir would say "Use discernment of spirit."

What that means is - understand when it is time to speak and tell the truth, and also when it is time to shut up, close your mouth, and not have conversations when there is no conversation to be had.

DISCERNMENT OF SPIRIT (example)

I felt like I had to give you an example because I truly don't want you running out here just speaking your mind all of the time, hurting others, causing discord, and then turning around and saying "Well WriterBoy said I should do this" NO! LOL

WriterBoy DID NOT!

To the parents, that boss you have, and co-workers that don't believe in you or your dreams, to the friends and family that may see you but may not see you if you get what I mean. To the people that say to you "Well how long are you going to do this until you stop?"

There is no conversation to be had. - Why continue to talk and have conversations when you know how they feel, you know who they are, and you know they will never believe in you how you want them to. Close your mouth, fix your eyes, dry your tears - it's time to get to work, you have a future to get.

For your partner, the one that you live with or even plan to build a life with, although they could be the "don't have a conversation" rule - they could also be the honest rule.

They could be the ones that I'm telling you to just be honest with and tell them how they've made you feel, tell them what I am looking for at this time is _____; telling them "at this moment you're not helping me at all"

It's just when you do that - be aware that sometimes honesty may cause friction, understand it, stand in it - and hope that your honesty provides clarity, understanding, and growth. But do not run away from it!

If you run - know that it will always catch up to you; your feelings will always be there; and no that it's either you keep it in for a lifetime as your unhappy - or you speak; and maybe things change, maybe things become different. It can be bad or good we don't know.

What we do know though is; you stay silent and let the pain eat you alive - the worst is guaranteed.

As I read that back to myself I'm thinking like - the old me would never do that - I would just walk away understanding that they just would never get it, I wouldn't speak I would carry on the truth with me and be hurt by every action they've done knowing I could just simply speak the truth, and maybe, just maybe they'll hear me.

I would walk away because of fear of causing discord, or fear of not being heard. - Choose your battles and not based off fear but based on love.

If you love a person, and you feel like clarity is something you guys shall need then I say do it, be honest - but if it goes left and clearly they cannot, will not, and have not heard you - you know what to do next - nothing. Stop having the conversation.

Why speak to someone that clearly can't hear you?

Hopefully I've made that clear.

With what has happened in our life another thing we can do to push forward and move into this future in our life is to

BE UNDERSTANDING

Understand that we are all human, understand that we are not alone, and understand that just as we have so much to unpack and go through, so does everyone else.

You are not the main character and main attraction of everyone else's movie, you're not the king or queen of everyone else's castle. The people that walk next to you day by day have their own castle, have their own queen, they are their own main characters in their world. They have their own problems.

I think we as humans quickly forget that we are not the only ones here, not the only ones on this planet. Sometimes we can be very selfish in thinking that the world must bend to us but then when it's time for us to bend to the world it's like

"How dare you ask me to do such a thing!?"

We're all human - we all are going through things - so the next time
someone is rude to you, or maybe they've said or did the wrong thing let's
just think

"Maybe they're having a bad day"
- just like we will next week, or that week after that, or the week after that.

Understanding that you're not the only one going through things in this
world no matter how things seem on the outside is a huge factor and stance
I think we all should have.

Be understanding and know that the person next to you is just like you,
they feel just like you feel, they hurt just like you hurt. - Their humans.
Now treat them how you want to be treated.

BE HERE

It's time for you to stop talking about the past and begin living in the present. I know that this is easier said than done but I didn't say it was going to be easy, I said that it needed to be done.

Right now I can hear you saying "who are you to tell me that I need to move on" and "you don't know what I've been through"

"Look where you're at! How could you possibly understand me?" "look at what you've come from"

Let me ask you, do you know where I've come from? No?

I grew up at a young age in a household where my mother and father argued to the top of their lungs every day! Screaming and fighting from one problem after the next; as this little boy I would run into the bathroom crying begging for them to stop. As I read this chapter back to myself, understanding that this is where some of my ideologies in life came from is shocking to me. Knowing that I felt like no one would ever hear me because they didn't hear me in these very traumatic moments in my life isn't a really good feeling. The feeling right now is like - it's time to let that little boy in the back of my head go. It's time for me to be here.

It was my mother sleeping in the same bed with me as I put my arms around her thinking that my little arm could protect her if my father came in the room to get her. This went on for about 1-2 years before they split but that was more than enough time for me to grow up for the next 2 decades believing that my voice could never be heard.

That little boy wanted peace in life (as a man he still does) that little boy cried for his voice to be heard - it never was, he was scared. This was his trauma.

Leaving that household, I grew up with my step-father that sold drugs out of our house. (mind you I'm not 69, he's done his time - were good yall) There were drugs, there was drug money, there were a lot of things that my mother didn't know I was even exposed to. I held a gun when I was 14. These are things that changed my outlook on life.

By the time I was 15 I began to be beaten by my stepfather behind my mother's back. He knew she wouldn't go for that, she never put her hands on me - so why would she let another human being on this earth do it to me. So he would wait - wait until she left for work to hit me, to beat me, to silence me, he would wait until she wasn't there.

He would wait - and he knew that I wouldn't speak, because I feared the discord that would come from my honesty. He knew that I wouldn't tell because I didn't want to break up our happy home.

I would cry to my grandmother who swore she would never tell my mother, and to my step sister who would always wonder why I wouldn't tell my mother.

One night when I didn't take out the trash - I remember sitting in the bathtub and my step father busting through the door, screaming at me, and slapping me so hard that my head went underwater.
I quickly rose up in so much embarrassment, in so much fear.
This was my trauma.

When I finally told my mother and she went off of course, protecting me, being there for me, but you know that didn't really help me - why because that's exactly what I feared! I did it . I sowed discord. My truth changed things - I was no longer seeing my step sister, we were back living with my grandmother. My words changed things.

Knowing that no one here's me and then when I do speak and I am heard my truth changes things …. was very scary to me. I was scared to speak. This was my trauma.

I'm not perfect, neither is my life. And this is not even half of the trauma I've been through in my life as a child growing up. These are just the ones I'm willing to talk about (and that should tell you something)

So how do I have the right to say it is time to let go of your past; because I've had my past - and just like you I'm telling myself right now - it is time to let go of your past. To speak and not be scared of the consequences of your truth.

It's time to move on from that scared kid that you were, that broken soul that you have. Because there is something so much greater waiting on the other side for you. You just can't grab it holding on to the past.

And hear me clearly it's not our fault, we did nothing wrong. - Our past happened to us not because of us.

It's just back then we didn't have a choice - but right now, this time we do. We can choose to stay attached to what used to be, what things were, who we used to be. - Or, or, we can move, we become who we were meant to be.

I can't stay in my past anymore, it's time for me to live in the present, it's time for us to be here - in the moment, right now.

//

REASON'S WHY NOT

🔊 **rea·son**
/ˈrēzən/

noun

1. a cause, explanation, or justification for an action or event.
    "the minister resigned for personal reasons"

    Similar: (cause) (grounds) (ground) (basis) (rationale) (motive) (⌄)

2. the power of the mind to think, understand, and form judgments by a process of logic.
    "there is a close connection between reason and emotion"

    Similar: (rationality) (logic) (logical thought) (scientific thinking) (reasoning) (⌄)

verb

think, understand, and form judgments by a process of logic.
"humans do not reason entirely from facts"

Similar: (think rationally) (think logically) (think straight) (use one's mind) (⌄)

So my best friend inspired this chapter. It was a quote Samir Zanders had said to me that has stuck with me every day since he said it. We both sat in my room – two manly men crying are tears out fighting to breathe and speak because of how hard we were crying (don't judge us) as I poured out my soul to my best friend for the past decade of how hard it has been for me to stand up and hold my head high as the enemy and the world continues to come crashing down on me.

I told him that it may seem like because I'm getting so much success that everything is just so amazing and peachy clean and it's not! It's a lot of hard work, a lot of stress, and dealing with a lot of people, a lot of anxiety.

Fighting the industry, fighting my friends, and now fighting even my family to give them something that it seems they don't even want. – But I digress.

As we cried I began to tell him that sometimes I just want to walk out of the house, wherever I'm at , I just want to go, just leave the front door and never come back; start all over, try a new life, a new me, a different me because I can't take this anymore.

Sometimes when you've fought for so long it feels like it's never going to end, it feels like it's always going to be something, it feels like you can't take it anymore. He began to ask me when I became so broken, when did I become so negative, so sad, so hurt.

Sometimes when you've fought for so long it takes a toll on you. But I can tell you this, you didn't come this far just to come this far. He said God would never give you anything you could not handle.

Me and my best friend sat in the room crying as I gave him all the reasons why I should give up. He sat up wiping his tears and began to tell me all of the things that I had accomplished, all of the fights that I have won, I listed all the reasons why I should give up, he began to list all of the reasons why I should never.

He told me of how I fought so hard, he told me about how I won so many times, and then I said to him

"If I'm really this man that God wants me to be why am I still falling down" his words that changed my life fierce were this

Crying he said

"You keep telling me how many times you fell down but have you stopped and counted how many times you've gotten back up"

Where I saw weakness my best friend see's all of me saw strength.

There is strength In not giving up, there is strength in not turning around. There is also strength in fighting for something that only you may believe in! There is strength in failure, there is strength in pain, there is strength in faith.

It takes a very strong individual to believe in something that you may not see yet. A strong individual to get back up when they've been knocked down time and time again. - It takes an incredible amount of strength for a person to hold the world on their shoulders as it laughs at you - knowing that one day, it'll all be worth it, they all will see. - They'll see me, they'll hear me, they'll understand me.

So to those reading this that have fallen, the moment you get back up you've taken back your power and your position as you have proven that you are strong.

Don't let the enemy trick you into thinking it's over, or you're done, or you should feel bad or broken. Don't let him tell you that you are not destined for everything and anything God has called you for - You may have fallen but you stood back up. And that's all that matters.

Know that There will always be a reason why you should give up, but for every reason why you there will always be a reason why not.

First reason is you have a purpose. There is a reason you are here in this lifetime and I know it hurts, and I know it's a lot; I know that sometimes it may feel like the end of the world, but it's not.

Sometimes it's just the beginning of a new chapter.

//

FIGHTING

FIGHT, v.i.

1. To strive or contend for victory, in battle or in single combat; to attempt to defeat, subdue or destroy an enemy, either by blows or weapons; to contend in arms.

I'm not going to lie, everything that I'm about to write in this chapter is easier said than done. But just because it's hard doesn't mean it's Impossible. To this day I still fight for peace in my life, I still fight for some type of sanity, I still fight to maintain what I have and I still fight for more.

As I write this chapter I've just fallen. - Yes I am who God says I am, yes I have more than what I've ever had before, and yes I am God's man, but - I'm still human. I think a lot of us dreamers believe that once you get to a certain place in life and you've learned so much and grown so much you will stop falling. I'm sorry to tell you that, that, just is not the case.

I can't tell you how many times I've fallen and called out to God asking him why! Why do I have to keep going through the same thing? Why do I have to keep fighting the same things!? Why do I have to keep falling!?

The answer to all of those questions is something very simple - I'm human. You are human, we are human; and because of that yes I will still make mistakes; because of that yes I will continue to fall down, and because of that yes I will continue to learn and grow. I don't think life was intended for us to ever be in a place where we stop growing, were we stop learning, where we stop moving.

For me I don't see God making people like us to be stagnant. I've realized that life is going to always have up and downs, peaks and valleys. Just knowing that I won't always be happy, I want always have the answers is something that I have to get used to. - Knowing that life won't be perfect.

I'm going to at least make it worth it. The ups and downs in life we can't choose to not have - but how we deal with them, how we move through life, and how find our happiness through the mindset of the store - that, that right there is the million-dollar question - I have a few answers to that. - We can't change the world around us, but we can definitely change who we are.

FALLING

Currently I'm in this transition phase; my family is growing, my career is growing, and it's time for me to rise up to the occasion and lead. All while I have distractions (Storms) all around me. I wish I didn't still have to go through this but like I previously stated. - this is something that we all must go through and not just as dreamers as people. We fall.

When I fall I begin to have doubt within myself, I begin to lose faith in myself, i begin to feel lost, i begin to feel - like me before God stepped in. And that's not a feeling I want to feel. I was 17 when God first began speaking to me and from there my life changed forever.

Before then I was just another young boy trying to find out who he was, what he wanted to do, and how he was going to get to wherever that was. With God he told me who I was, he told me the man I would be, and gave me a road map on how to get to that man. - Why would I trade all of that for anything in this world?

But yet I do time and time again. I fall and I fall hard. - I've prayed about it, I cried about it all, I've even fought over the decision to continue to allow drama, pain, hurt, and the whispers of my failure in my life.

I know by now you're saying how can you have written all of these guidelines and rules to help a dreamer if you're still falling yourself.

I smile as I write this because this is something I just came to the realization of and had to come back and write......

You will fall; as a dreamer you will fall, as a human being you will fall. You fall at the worst times, you fall right before your breakthroughs, you will fall right after you pass a goal, you will fall right before you get through that goal.

But it's not about how many times you have fallen like my best friend said, it's about that strength that you have that for some reason you keep standing back up; time and time again Some people give up after falling, there's a reason you haven't

Picking up this book means you have strength, you're more than the average person, if you have strength to LEARN how to fight for what you want in life you have strength enough to ACTUALLY DO IT. So when it becomes time, or if it is time right now, do it, fight for what you want; it's time to stand up.

For the past couple of days, I began listening to TD Jakes over and over and over again. It's a sermon I listened to a long time ago that really helped me understand the place I was in life. It helped me make that change that was needed from me.

His words were "There's nothing more powerful than a changed mind." When I first heard this I didn't quite understand it but it's something every dreamer religion or not should hear; it will give you the true definition of change, the true definition of your mind and what it means to be whole.

After listening to the video years ago I decided to become a vegetarian (lol) yeah I know that doesn't make any type of sense and had literally nothing to do with the sermon, but let me tell you why I did it.

A lot of times we can't believe things until we see them. I wanted to prove to myself that I have self-control, mind, body, and soul, so I decided to start with my body - if I can control the outside of me then I know I can control the inside of me. I stopped eating meat, all meat. This way I knew I'm in control, not what I crave, not what I want – but me, Brandon, I wanted to know that I have control over my mind, my body, and my soul.

It's been almost 6 years now that I haven't eaten meat. To be honest It's been an amazing journey and has taught me so much about myself and within myself. I learned that I could control my mind. I mean I learned that in the first 6 months but me being me after I started this journey in life there was no going back, I had to finish it.

My point of it all is that I learned that I was in control - that this is my life, and the outcome of who I am is a result of my actions, and not anyone's else.

This is something that although I did a long time ago I must relearn, sometimes I'm quick to forget that I'm in control; because this world really does make it seem like the storms around us are our lives, this world makes it seem like the fight is really all there is to it - but it's not; and sometimes I have to take a step from the storm and remember who I am.

Just like a car if you drive it for years, if you've went over hundreds of speed bumps, dirt roads, drove it through storms, and horrific weather, it's still your car, it's still you; sometimes you just need to take it to the shop, get some things tightened up, get those wheels realigned.

There's nothing wrong with re-teaching your mind. Relearning what you once knew. There's nothing wrong with falling, down, getting back up, and re teaching your mind how to never do that again.

IT'S OKAY TO NOT BE OKAY

//

DEPRESSION

Today was a very hard day for me. Before I start this part of the chapter I just want to let you know it's okay to not always be okay. Depression is something that I never thought I would have to deal with; it's also not something you just get over, or you can just wash away by saying it will be okay; yes, it will be, but sometimes as a dreamer, no, as a person you don't want to hear it will be okay. You don't want to hear that everything is going to be okay.

It's funny because as I write this down I know that it is the truth, I know I will be okay, this too shall pass but sometimes it's just much easier to lay down and give up than it is to stand up and fight.

Fighting is hard, and it's long, it's an uphill battle and sometimes I just get tired of fighting like I know you do, but if you're like me you don't want to just settle for anything else in life, you don't want to settle for where you are now - so do what I'm about to do – get up, and fight.

I don't want to - I don't feel like it. I feel like laying down and crying, curling up into a ball and just leaving. Right now - I feel like walking out of this door and never coming back like I said before! Starting an entire new life, I feel like giving up.

The key words in all that is "feel" everything I've just stated is how I feel. And if you don't know, feelings can change in an instance, a second, a minute. Feelings are temporary. And I won't make a permanent decision based on temporary circumstances.

So turn on your favorite song, listen to your favorite speaker, or pastor, don't have one find one and listen to them. At this moment do not allow the enemy or the world to have your mind; Begin to listen and surround yourself with positivity! If you have to step away from your friends, your family, find a place in your mind where you can lock yourself in and be at peace – DO THAT!
Don't allow the world to have your mind.

I would never say I suffer from something because then I claim it. What I will say however is that I've been depressed before and it's not fun, it's not funny and it hurts. To feel like no one has you, to feel like no one hears you. To feel like no one will ever understand you. To know that this world makes it so hard to be happy. It's hard.

But you see me, I will not sit in it, I will not sit in my pain and misery because it is not what I was created to do.

I will not lay down and just take all of the hurt and pain that this world is giving me. I'm not just going to lay here and take it. I'm going to fight, I'm gonna get up and fight even harder than I have ever fought before! Why, because I wanna go, I wanna get out, I want more out of life. And I want to be heard

People cry and lay down because they don't want to be there, me I cry and fight my way through, for the same exact reason.

It hurts, but which one will you do? In life there will always be something against you, it just feels like the closer you get to your dream the harder those somethings become.

Smiled again writing this because I think every obstacle I've been through in life I thought was the end; and now looking back like it wasn't even that serious. Getting through depression takes time but don't sit in it, get up and fight for your mind.

Whether it's sitting still and finding your peace, taking your time and finding God, or taking the time out of your day to find you next step.

I don't think no one wants to be depressed. I do think a lot of people were broken down, pushed down and they don't want to have the strength to fight back, they want to find the strength to get back up, people are tired of fighting! I'm tired of fighting.

ENOUGH IS ENOUGH

Sometimes when you're pushed into a corner and you feel like you've just had enough of everyone! Your family, your friends, your life; it's not a bad thing, it's okay, I know you're mad, I know you're tired. - get tired. You stand up even if you're mad, you stand up even if you don't want to. I don't care what it looks like, I don't care who you are, stand up.

Today I cried on the bathroom floor. Ironic huh? The person that you think has it all is on the bathroom floor crying, feeling not only alone but depressed. Surrounded by people chasing his dreams and still hurting and fighting to stand up! Why you ask, because I'm fighting for something that is more than myself. - but at this moment it has become so much on my back that I question if any of this is worth the hurt and pain on my mind. Is it worth all that I am going through?

Right now I'm in a bad place; why because I chose to allow the world around me in. And it sucks, while everyone that's helped push me into this corner is out smiling have a good time I sit on a deflated air mattress writing to you guys. - Why can a person that knows so much end up in the same place as everyone else? - Because we all fall. I guess.

I choose not to speak because I don't always believe in humans, and then the moment I put trust in them they fail me. That's why I trust myself, I love myself, I would never distrust myself.
Moral of the story - fight, don't be like me right now.

Entry: March 19th 2019 at 12:35pm

Day 2:

So today I'm going to tell you something I've told few people. I dream of running away. *(You've heard this already but listen to how I though, and understand the lesson of where I was at in this moment)* I dream of leaving out of the house that I'm in and just running off. Leaving behind this life and starting something different.

I know your probably reading this like how? And why? But everyday being surrounded by a world that just takes from you is not only draining its hurtful, it's depressing, everyone needs something from you, they call they want something, they come they want something and the moment you need something from the world your returned with nothing.

But I've found that the reason I sit in this dark place is because I've put my trust in the world and others around me vs putting my trust in God.

If you go and search up the song "I need you now" by Smokie Norful these are the words I'm saying to God at this moment and my exact feelings. Mind you if you're in this dark place it will make you cry, yes, but it will also give you a bit of peace, and some type of strength, it gives you hope, and so much more.

At this moment I feel lost and undecided - I feel broken. And I don't know how to fix myself. I've never wanted to give up more in my life than at this moment. I've given the world all of me and the world has given me nothing back.

How do you not run from a world that hurts you?
This is a fight that I don't even think I wanna fight anymore.

Coming back in 2022

Know that this little boy did things that God didn't ask him to do, gave things God never asked him to give. - God never told me to lean on the world, he told me to lean on him. God never told me to trust in this world, he told me to trust in him. -

God had never told me to give my heart to the world, he told me to give my heart to him. - There lies my mistakes. I won't always have peace but I will always have him - he'll provide that & more for me.

HEARTBREAK

So this part of the book I'm really not too fond of writing, to be honest I wasn't prepared to write this - it's just happened. Sometimes when you're transitioning in life things are going to change, things that you want to change, and others that you don't. You have to take the good with the bad and know that your future is worth it all.

In each and every one of your relationships you will learn something, even with me I've always learned from the things that I've gone through, whether it be 5 months or 5 years to leave with nothing but pain and sorrow would be insane, unaccountable, and a waste of your precious time, energy, and space on earth. Learn something from these experiences.

Transitioning to the next phase in your life will definitely be hard but just like every storm, every battle, and every fight that you've been up against before - you will definitely get through this one.

For me - I begin by one remembering who I was before the relationship, who I am now, and finally who I will be after.

A lot of people are so scared to be alone but I remember a quote from someone I saw online who said "If you don't even wanna be with yourself, what makes you-think somebody else will." lol It is the truth; but beyond that - start taking care of you instead of waiting on the next person to do so, no one is going to treat you like you wanted be treated, no one is going to love you how God loves you, and no one's going to give to you the way you will give to yourself.

So instead of looking for the world to take care of you and love you, begin doing those things for yourself. Even if it's taking a walk in the park, taking a drive down the road, working out, going to get something to eat, hell watching a movie.

All I'm saying is - treat yourself right. For a long time I've been beating myself up, treating myself bad, treating my body bad, I've not cared about myself, what makes me think the world is going to care about me, let alone should care about me.

It's time for me to stop treating the world better than I treat yourself. And you should do the same, stop giving the world everything as it gives you nothing in return. - Now that don't mean you go out there cursing people out, stepping over people, or hurting other, becoming the person or the people that continue to hurt you - what it means is this:

You ever heard the saying "treat people how you wanted to be treated?"

Well, let's add something to this saying.

"Treat people how you want to be treated **AND treat yourself how you want the world to treat you.**"

When you're going through things like this in life I know you have so many questions in your head like "Oh God or why this, and why that," "God why did you have me!" but let's push through the sorrow and pain and let's start asking the right questions.

It's not about why this is happening, it's about what comes from this, it's about what comes after this.

I must be human for you to understand me. I get that now.

I want to make something clear before I continue. What God has for you is for you! Your dream, your future, your destiny belongs to you and only you! God will never deliver the right package to the wrong door!

I want you to know that your destiny does not expire in 2 weeks, nor in two months, or in two years or even a decade. Forget what they've told you, forget what you've heard, forget what they've said - what has God said about you? What God has for you?

What God has for you will never expire, you just have to keep walking.

It was a time where me and King Vader, my client, my artist, most importantly one my best friends in this entire world and truly one of my biggest supporters. Since we were kids it's been me and Vader.

If you ask Vader it was me that started all of this, that installed all this into him, I've said it to him before but I don't think he heard me.

Because yes our lives may have started with me picking up that camera, forcing him to stay up with me, writing, editing, filming; his dream had become an extension of mines and watching him become everything he wanted to be, helping him do everything he said he wanted to do, watching him jump time and time again it is because of Vader that I knew that my words could change people, It's because of him that I knew my words could change the world,

His first award Vader received on stage I cried on the side as he stared at me and said

"I know you're going to change the world WriterBoy, I'm just happy you started with mine."

I always wanted him to know It is because of King Vader that WriterBoy knows he can change the world.

As I was growing in this film Industry I met this amazing man named Mikael Moore, an Executive, Writer, Producer, and among all of the amazing things he does he still finds time to manage Pop Artist and Icon Jannel Monae.

I remember pitching films to him fresh into this industry and him loving them, him telling me what was needed, him guiding me on the business side of things before walking me into rooms.

He was one of many men in this industry that would help me on my journey to becoming who I was, who I am. And not just on the business side, but more importantly personally.

Backing up to me and Vader; We work hard, we don't sleep, we eat few, and fight for more. We're working our butts off even more than usual! We were coming up and I promise you all eyes were on us! We had to win!

We had Warner Brothers in our back pocket, Amazon, LeBron's James Production Company, everyone was looking at these two black boys wondering saying they can make films. What are they about to do?

So yes, I began working myself to death, in all shapes, sizes, and forms, I wasn't eating like I should have been, sleeping pretty much at all, and I was stressing myself out with all of the worries I ever had. Around that time RDC world was at Airbnb and it seemed like me and Mark and I were on the same page, it's now or never!

I remember it being my birthday and I was in bed sick - yup, sick. With dark circles around my eyes, drugged out from all of the Benadryl I was taken, dark circles around my eyes, skin itching, it was not a good site; to top it all off I had to deliver a pitch deck for our film to Mikal the same day. I was done for it.

I remember getting on a call with him apologizing for the delay and telling him that I'm going to give it to him as soon as I could.

He asked

"Brandon, are you good?"

I told him I was fine; I've just been sick for a while. - Mikal paused and then began to tell me a story about one of his friends who was a DJ and a producer. He said to me

"Brandon, he worked his ass off to get to where he wanted, and he got there - but he also got really sick getting there."

He began to tell me how his friend is bed ridden and how all of the riches and success that he had made meant nothing to him now knowing that he could never enjoy it.

He then said to me

"Do you believe that if you don't get whatever you're chasing now you will never get it, do you think it's now or never."

I told him

"Absolutely! I don't have anything else, this is my all, this is all I have, it's me and this dream. It really is now or never"

Ladies and gentlemen his response to me would change the course of my life forever; he said

"If you truly believe you are who you say you are, Brandon, it's never going to be now or never, it's now or tomorrow. "

I understood.

I hope you do too. Your dream, no, your destiny, is not going anywhere anytime soon. So yes, work your butt off, fight for everything you want in life, dream and dream big - but don't hurt yourself where you won't even be able to enjoy the fruits of your labor.

Work hard. Fight harder - but don't kill yourself.

And know if you are who you say you are - you're going to get there - and no that doesn't mean sit on your ass and do nothing - it means work, fight, but when it's half time, when it's a break, and when the round is over, you rest. That dream of yours is not going anywhere anytime soon; because it belongs to you.

It's not now or never, it's now or tomorrow!

PLAN

I was 18 when I began filming my first feature film EVER! 18-year-old

Brandon with his amazing mind, and his amazing dream in his match box

room, in one of the hardest hoods in DC took the train to staples (which I

want you to do) doesn't have to be the train but GET UP AND GO TO

THE STORE - If you want to be spontaneous let's do it right now; get up

and take my book with you. - Finish reading my words when you get there.

If you're there or you're going later that's fine - now I want you to do what

I did when you get there. Grab sticky notes, markers and thumbtacks.

When I got home from buying all of those things on the first note I wrote

what I wanted to accomplish.

I remember to this day, it said "Premiere Adapt in a Theater" i then began

writing on each sticky note after the things I needed to accomplish in order

to get there, the smallest details to the biggest ones, (finish script,

copyright it, trademark name, get film team, do casting call, ect.) each

moment will have a sticky note.

An 18 year old boy then got his bed and then began moving it around his

room and sticking the stick notes at the bridge of the wall around my entire

room and in order of which it needed to be done first.

As I began my journey I worked hard to accomplish these moments, each goal I achieved I snatched the note down off the wall! One goal at a time.

I smile as I write that almost a year later after doing this that 18-year-old boy premiered his film in a theater. Yes, I added more goals under the big goals as I went along the way but I accomplished those too and then continued with the others. I did it, and you will too. Go get the notes, write down your goals, and stick them on your wall so in order of operation.

It is very important that you follow each of my steps to the t. Each sticky note must have one goal on it; the sticky notes behind must be the goals building up to that sticky note in front of them or they must be in order of operation. No matter how small or big the goal, write it down.

You must also pull the sticky notes down off the wall once you've completed them in life. Now I know it feels to you like you're throwing away your accomplishments but you're not - you're moving past them! A goal is not meant to stay on your wall forever.
The reason you're putting them on there is so that you can take them down one day.

If you must keep them, buy a small trash can for them and when you take them off the wall throw them in there. Watch the can fill up; watch your wall clear up.

Another reason for taking them down is because waking up to all of those dreams and goals on the wall day in and day out could give a person high anxiety with all of those notes. But waking up to a wall where empty spaces lay where goals and dreams did is an amazing feeling

Seeing your goals left next to space where goals achieved once laid is an amazing feeling! And that dopamine you're going to feel when you pull that sticky note off the wall and throw it in the trash is going to feel so good. I promise you

So follow my instructions, write your goals down, put them on the wall, and as you tear them off, watch the smile on your face as you bring your dreams to reality, as you make your world come to life.

These are some of the tools I used to find my dreams, now let me give you the journey I went through to find my peace.

FINDING YOUR PEACE

02/09/2019 – 4:14 am

I'm currently on a mission to find the answers to a problem that we all have. The problem is simple; Keeping your mind, finding your peace, how do we as dreamers; no, we as humans stay sane in this dark world that wants to drive us insane.

I've found that what you want in life, the world makes it hard to obtain, and what you fear the most is what it gives to you on a silver platter. How do we as humans get through the hardships, maintain our strength, and maintain our peace in a world willing to give us hell in an instant.

At first I thought it was having a significant other – but see that's flawed in its own. Sometimes they help in bringing your chaos; I think we all can agree on that.

At one point I even though it may be the love of a parent maybe the mother or father that could help keep you sain but in most cases they are the ones that help push you over the edge as well, and if your blessed to have a mother like mines that actually supports you the nagging of everything will flip you right off the edge with everyone else (lol).

Their mom's their dads, no matter how much support they give or don't, please remember that they're human just like you, they feel just like you, and they're going nag. kick. and scream if they love you, why? Because they love you.

But that still doesn't answer my question. If it's not the love of someone else that will bring me peace, if it's not the love from my parents that will bring me peace, then what is it? Where is our peace? Where is the answer to one of the biggest problems of them all?

I know that we all will always have problems of course. Me being around these people high up in the industry and even surrounded by celebrities there's one thing I can tell you – No one is perfect.

No matter the money, no matter the status, no matter how far you've come or how hard you fought - no one is perfect.

So once again, we all will always have problems; but where does our peace lie within that; and how do we maintain that peace?

I've asked all around, my friends, my colleagues, my circle, and a lot of people of very generic answers, they workout, they pray (which is definitely needed to get through this world – a must do), Other just focus on work, and then there's me – trying to control everything in my world because I know if I'm in control nothing can go wrong. – So what happens when all of my control is taken away from me. – I lose my entire head.

I'm not looking for generic answers to my question. – The question of how to not lose your peace requires more than a simple answer; it's supposed to be a list. Tools you can use to continue to strive for more in life, reach for better than what you have and who you are.

It's a list of weapons you can use in your battle for your mind, body, and soul. – As I write this I still continue to think – what is the answer to this question in my head. – How do I keep my peace?

In all honesty guys I'm a little disappointed in myself right now, usually I have all the answers – and right now with one of the most important questions of them all I can't seem to find it.

Maybe I can't find the answer because I've been searching for it in everyone else's life but although we're all fighting for the same future all of our lives are very different in many ways. – Maybe the answer to this specific question is different for each specific person.

Let's try something, in the next few pages I'm going to begin to list the things that I've been going through that have been causing me to lose my mind. – Maybe if I can see the problem I can then find the solution.

Hear me out – You can solve a math by first drawing it out on paper, then you follow up the necessary steps breaking down steps by step to your solution – and finally you follow it up with the answer to the equation. I think I just made everything I said sound way more complicated than it is - but let's try this.

My Problems.

1. My family doesn't understand that I'm trying to help them, I feel like at this moment I'm fighting my family more than I'm fighting for them.

2. I feel like I've been too kind to too many people, I feel like the world is on my shoulders and as I carry it the people around me smile like "You're WriterBoy" you got this.

So once again I'm laughing because as I began writing down my problems I realized that I didn't really have a lot of problems – at least none that are so serious that I should be losing my entire mind over. If I wanted to be petty and make myself feel bad I could go on and on about my life and the pain and misery that's in it but I began to feel myself reaching for things in the back of my mind to be hurt over, & I think a lot of us do that.

Sometimes when things go wrong in our worlds we begin to pile on one thing after another, after another; making the pain, the sorrow, and the story of being in pain and down and out worse than it even is. – Why do we do that? Do we like pain, do we like misery, or is it the simple fact that we got knocked down and we honestly just don't have the energy to get back up, Or maybe we just want to talk and sit on the floor for a minute, take us a breathe before we have to get back up and fight.

Everyone isn't like me, so I know some people like to sit there, some just get back up, some talk and then get up, and then there are others – others that leave because of all of the pain and depression the world has thrown at them.

The point I'm trying to make is to pick and choose your battle. You don't have to add more opponents to the ring, of course you're going to lose when it's 10 on 2! you get to choose how many people you want to fight and who and what's worth it.

So here we go, I've chosen my (2) I'll give you your chance. What are the two main problems in your life? Write them down – Just so that you can see them front and center on paper.

WRITE YOUR PROBLEMS DOWN

RIGHT NOW! RIGHT HERE!

Now that you've listed your problems, let's find our solutions. For me the first solution of mine is simple, 1. stop fighting with my family. – I'm making the decision to get into the ring and fight with them, it takes two to tango and I'm stepping in the ring just like they are, and that's not who I am. – I want to help them, yes, but should it be at the cost of losing who I am? – No. So for now no more fighting.

2. I found that sometimes being a strong human being a lot of people don't come to your aid because you don't look defenseless, you look and speak as if you can handle yourself - and you can; but sometimes back would be much appreciated right. The next line I'm about to say is very harsh but true - People will always fail you. They will, their human, were all flawed and we all fail at some point. With that being said - it is truly your job to take care of you! No one is coming to save you, if they do, congratulations! If they don't? Take out your cape, put on your mask, and save your damn self.

Don't take on more than you can bare, learn to say no EVEN THOUGH I know it's hard you must do it, and truly that even if you don't see humans standing by your side - God will always be there.

Now let's step back just a little. I asked a question at the beginning of all this, that question was "How do you keep your peace?" It's been almost a week since I had my last entry here, and the answer to my question has finally been given. – See, I knew I could figure It out.

I don't believe this world was meant to push us forward and towards our dreams, goals, and ambitions in life. I actually think that it's set up to do the complete opposite. And this – is coming from WriterBoy the guy that has "made it"

Straight to the point – if this world we live in wasn't meant to give you your dreams nor your peace, why do you constantly look for the world to give you either?

Whether it's your family or your friends, co-workers, or your school. You look at the world for acceptance, for happiness, for peace, you want people to treat you nice and do nice things for you, to you, because of you -, sometimes when you're a good person, a good human being you expect others to be good to you – you expect this world to be good to you. – And that's just not how this works.

We are all human, and we are all flawed. We all make mistakes in life. Just like you, you must understand that people are human.

A friend of mines once told me to stop putting expectations on my friends, to stop putting expectations on my family. – The reason is because time and time again they will fail, they will always fail. – Because they are human, and putting these high expectations on people that are just trying to figure it out just like you, no matter how old they are, or how long they've been here

Is unreasonable and can causes a lot of conflict, grief, hurt, and despair in your life just because you expected more from others and they didn't give that to you.

I want you to try this exercise with me. Take a deep breath and close your eyes, picture yourself sitting on a body of water watching a waterfall come down from huge mountains. – Suddenly the waterfall begins to split and you start to see a man or woman begin to walk out through the middle of that waterfall.

As they get closer and closer to you he or she is revealed to be an older version of who you are.

What do you see? Who do you see? What do you look like?

How do you feel?

Now, how do you become them? What are your solutions to your problems? We always think about the problems, that's easy to do, but what are the solutions? What next, what's your next step, your next goal, how do you get out of where you are and get to where you're going, and don't tell me there is no way; there is always a way. It may be hard, it may not be what you want, but there's always a way to get up, anytime you've fallen.

People are human so forgive them, have understanding for others, have understanding for yourself, fight through the hurt, forgive, and let go, it's time to become that person that you see in that waterfall, it's time to let go, time to move on, it's time for more. - Besides you have work to do.

WRITE YOUR SOLUTIONS DOWN

RIGHT NOW! RIGHT HERE!

BECOMING RADICAL

Are you willing to do whatever it takes to get your dream? Even if that means becoming someone else? – Even if it means becoming uncomfortable. Because that's exactly what it will take.

At a certain time in your life you will have to make a decision on if you will be the person your friends, your parents, and your world wants you to be, or if you will be who you want to be!

Coming into this world, into this industry, I found myself wanting the entire world to like me, wanting to be there for people, like God was for me, wanting to teach people like God taught me. – that's even why I wrote this book, I want to help as many people as I can.

But – In my case, giving all of yourself to the world, and leaving none for God and you – isn't and shouldn't be an option for you. You – must take care of you. And I know that it is hard sometimes when you want everyone around you to be okay but you cannot make sure that the world is okay if you're not here to do so. So I start this chapter off by saying this. – It's time for you to be radical.

Now I'm not saying that it's going to be easy, nor am I saying that it's going to happen overnight BUT what I'm saying is it must happen!

In the bible for those who read it. It says "Protect Your Heart" if you're reading this book you want more out of life you may even want more for others – but before you can change the world you must change this part of yourself as well.

When I say radical I do not mean to be mean, nor nasty towards others, I am not saying to hurt others with your actions or words. – I am telling you to be blunt, to be bold; to hold yourself accountable of how people treat you – and how you treat you, and what you do about it.

People only treat you – how you allow them to. If they scream and you do nothing they now know to scream at you. – If they hit you and you turn away they now know to hit you. If they scream your name and you turn, they now know how to get your attention. Teach people how to treat you – and with that comes being radical.

This message is something it took me a very long time to learn and still to this day now 25 years old I'm still learning it. You want to know how I broke out of my fear of being radical? – it was my son.

He has been acting up at school, at home, and I got a call from his mother stating a lot of things that he's been not only feeling but acting out. Now mind you Isiah is not that type of child, at 11 years old he is one of the brightest and most amazing little guys I've ever met, he's going to be somebody amazing one day. I really believe it.

Nevertheless, I had to have a hard conversation with him that I did not want to have. His mother called me and I needed to say something to this amazing guy that's not acting so amazing right now. I knew I needed to be radical and say the things I didn't want to say to him, I honestly didn't want him to hurt.

I asked him who I was talking to
"because the Zay I know doesn't act like this"

I said to him that I don't respect it at all
"We don't disrespect none of our parents – ever"

I then told him.
"I'm disappointed in you"

The moment I said those words one of my favorite guys in the world began to cry and I turned the camera as I started tearing up, because I never want to hurt him, and I just did. But I understood he needed to hear the honesty for him to know what to do and what not to do. I needed to be honest with him.

Now call me what you want but I could never hurt any of the 5 god children I have and walk away feeling like I'm okay. – If you can do that you're a psychopath, stay away from all of my kids.

II had to fight through what I wanted to do and do what I had to do to make sure this kid wakes up the next day knowing that he hasn't been acting like himself. He wakes up the next day to change himself, to mold himself; to have a better life than what he was creating himself.

I had to be blunt, I had to be bold, I had to be honest, WriterBoy had to be radical. – By the way, he's doing amazing in school, and I'm taking him to my house to cook and talk to me the moment my flight lands in DC.

I had to understand that his feelings would be hurt but his life would be better. And, if I could do that to an 11-year-old boy, why am I not doing that to the world?

One of my best friends Devonate Dockery tried to teach me this when we were younger. It was his constant picking at me for the whole truth, the whole reason why, my whole opinion and not just half of it. He pushed me to tell the truth and the whole truth to him just as he had done with me. He wanted me to speak and know that what I say does matter, even if it hurts sometimes, it's okay.

To this day he still knows when I'm giving him a half answer or half-truth because I don't want to hurt anyone and he's quick to fast forward and be like:

"So you don't like it - okay, that's all you had to say, Brandon just talk."

Sometimes I feel like I'm trying to protect the world around me, when in reality, you're not protecting the world, you're hurting it, you're hurting them by not stepping up to the plate and saying the truth because you are scared of how people may portray you. Speak.

Today I hopped on a phone call and had to be radical with two people. – I did it and guess what the outcome was – they apologized, they understood, and they told me that it would never happen again.

And if it does, I will address any situation again, and teach people that "No" you will not speak to me in any kind of way. "No, you will not treat me in any kind of way and "Yes" you can get up from my table if you do not like what is being served." Again Discernment of Spirit; know when to speak and when not to.

Every time someone does you wrong or says the wrong thing to you does not mean you run out there and start a war. - Speak if they mean something to you, speak if this relationship is intended to last a long time, speak if the conversation will truly matter. If not, don't.

If you know you're a good person and put good out into the world. Do exactly what I'm about to tell you to do.

Be the love and protection you so desperately seek others to be for you, to you. Be Radical.
And if you're already that – let's not take it too far, protect your space, protect your energy, protect others. – Do what you have to do, But don't be an ass whole.

Yes, standing on your own voice may be hard sometimes but trust me it's worth it. If you speak up for yourself, if you tell the world how it is, if you protect yourself and your space on a day to day basis this chapter is not for you.

This chapter is for those with a voice they do not use it, those being seen and never heard, this is chapter for those voices that our silent yet have so much to say.

Don't hold your truth in, speak it, and if they understand amazing, and if they don't at least you did all you can do to give them understanding you.

Speak

Say it out loud for me

"Speak"

I keep going over this chapter in my head because I hope that I've made myself very clear! When you speak, you speak out of love; when you talk, you with purpose, and when you move, be guided with your motions.

Speak, but in ways the world or that person can understand.

Everybody won't make it.

You want to know how to get to your dream right? How to make your dream a reality – let me simplify this entire book.

1. Keep to yourself, don't tell the world that doesn't even see you, dreams that they can't see.

2. Understand your worth, understand you're an amazing person and that you and your dream are worth millions, don't oversell or undersell yourself, don't let anyone tell you that you are not worth it or not good enough, not even me.

3. Fight, Fight for what you want in life, fight for what you believe in, fight for a message, and fight yourself.

4. Lastly, never give up – don't give up on yourself or your dream, don't take the easy way out, I promise you it'll be worth the journey.

Know that you're not perfect, Know that life's not perfect, and know the problems won't go away, problems will always be there. It's up for you to learn RIGHT HERE RIGHT NOW! How to evolve and maneuver around those problems and storms that may come into your life.

STANDING IN YOUR OWN WAY

This part of my journey is for those very smart, very intelligent people like me that think too much, too fast, too soon. Sometimes we tend to get in our own way. We over think, we over plan, and we over shadow our own thoughts and our voice sometimes.

I want you to know that one, you are not God, you can't stop what he wants to happen, two, you're not that important, the universe does not end where you begin. Maybe knowing that will help you make decisions more clearly. lol. It did for me - it allowed me to know that the buck doesn't stop with WriterBoy. Also knowing that it's not the end of the world. Make your decision, and keep it moving - life doesn't stop and not even for you.

Lastly it was for me to listen to God and God only and stop trying to do things on your own - it's helped me stop overthinking things, just ask the question, be guided by his answers, and hopefully just hopefully I won't be in my mind because I'm too busy doing what he has for me to do in this world.

Moral of the story if you know that sometimes you can be in yours in your own head, stay out of it. Why be the villain in your story that you do not need? If God thought you needed something to push you more towards him or the destiny he has for you, trust and believe he would have sent something your way. - He didn't because he doesn't, and he also doesn't need your help.

Go sit down, take a drink, and mind your business - God has you and he doesn't need your help.

FOCUS

🔊 **fo·cus**

/ˈfōkəs/

See definitions in:

(All) (Geology) (Medicine) (Physics) (Mathematics) (Linguistics)

noun

1. the center of interest or activity.
   "this generation has made the environment a focus of attention"

   Similar: (center) (focal point) (central point) (center of attention) (hub) (pivot) (⌄)

2. the state or quality of having or producing clear visual definition.
   "his face is rather **out of focus**"

   Similar: (focal point) (point of convergence) (sharp) (crisp) (distinct) (clear-cut) (⌄)

verb

1. (of a person or their eyes) adapt to the prevailing level of light and become able to see clearly.
   "try to **focus on** a stationary object"

2. pay particular attention to.
   "the study will focus on a number of areas in Wales"

Before we begin talking about ways that we must and will become focused let's talk about all the ways in which we can become distracted.

1. The work in front of us. Some days the work we have doesn't match the work that shall be. Meaning the tasks that we have aren't for the future nor are they pushing us towards our future- these things that we do on a day to day basis are only for right now, for the needs of this moment - and that's okay.

    Where it becomes a problem is when we are only worrying about now and never looking towards the future. - Just living for now. You'll hear me say this throughout my entire life, with everything you've learned in this book and more you must have "Balance"

    It's a must. You must balance between now and then. You must balance between work and sleep, you must balance between fight and rest, you must balance between loving someone and loving yourself, - there must always be balance.

2. People, places, things - the grass will always and forever look greener on the other side - until you step in it and it's just a lot of paint and dirt that has turned into mud. - or the grass is just simply fake. My point is - don't be distracted by the things around you.

    The places that you see nor the people that you hear speak. No one is perfect, nothing is perfect, and no one's life is perfect. You have a job to do, a position to feel in this world. You have somewhere to be, someone to be, don't be confused or distracted, don't be blinded by the sun touching the fake green grass - continue to plant your seeds and water them all.

    The sun is coming and I promise it's for you.

3. Do not get complacent or comfortable. I can tell you first-hand how the moment you begin to get a taste of your success - which you will, you can lose sight of the bigger picture at times as you will start to see the shiny grass growing on your own lawn, you forget the mud and dirt that was once laid there and start forgetting to water it. You become comfortable because you finally see the green grass. You'll say

"It can go one day without water" or ' I'll get it tomorrow" or the next day.

Don't wait until tomorrow, don't wait until the next day, don't sit down or sit around because it's started to grow, get up and get to work because how you got there is how you're going to get even further.

Your grass has grown and that's what's up, don't you want it to grow more, get greener, spread to the backyard? Yes? Then get to work. DON'T STOP WATERING! DON'T GET COMFORTABLE. Don't stop growing! You have work to do.

This is the beginning of your future, not the start, not the middle, not the end, no matter how you feel. You haven't reached the ceiling … you're just getting started, get back to work. Focus is not something you just have, it's something you push yourself to do. For example, you continue to read this book, me continuing to write this book; us both continuing to find not only meaning in life but fight for more in life.

The point I'm trying to make is Focus isn't something you have, it's something you do. You must focus, you must stay focused, and when, not if, but WHEN you do fall you must get back up and regain your focus.

I had a dream years ago when I was around 19-20 years old. In this dream I was walking into a movie theater, it was very empty but all of the aisles were filled with bushes.

In this dream I was walking straight as each aisle full of bushes stood taller than me on my right and left. As I walked towards what was at the end of the theater things started to come out of the bushes pushing and pulling me right and left.

I remember being so scared but still wanting to make it to the end, I remember feeling like they can't stop me. All they can do is delay me, so I have to keep going, I have to stay focused, I can't lose sight of what is in front of me.

I remember getting up the next day and feeling like it was time to not be distracted, it was time for me to get to work.

I want you to understand me truly and purely. At 17 years old when God began speaking to me, guiding me, working with me it was one scripture not that I read but they told me about; it was a story about a man walking on water.

He told me about Peter leaving the boat as he walked towards him on water, he told me about the storm that arose during the man walk, the people yelling for him to come back into the boat. He told me how Peter looked away and slowly began to sink. Ye with little faith.

On this journey in life there will be many storms that come to pass, that I promise you. On this journey in life, people will not always understand you, they fear the storm, they will fear you drowning, they will kick and scream for you to get back on that boat.

That's because they don't see what you see, they don't see that you're walking towards God, towards your future, towards your destiny. All they see is the storm but you, you see more.

So don't turn around because of the loud screams that are around you, don't be scared of the storm that grows near you, stay focused on him and only him. Focus on all that he has for you.

The bible Peter looked away from God and at the storm and began to sink; Jesus walked up to him pulling him from out of the water and said to him

"Ye with little faith"

I don't want to drown, and I don't want to fall short in front of the ones that I love. So I must focus, I must stay consistent, I must keep my eyes on God and only God, because if I don't
I'll sink, and I don't want to sink.

//

HAVING CONVERSATIONS:

Growing up I was taught not to have conversations where there is no conversation to be had. – What does this mean? It means that if a person truly isn't going to hear you, truly isn't going to agree with you, and will never understand you, why are you having a conversation with them.

You keep telling your dreams to people that will never understand you, hoping that they get it, praying that they see it, and when it doesn't happen you walk away feeling hurt, beaten, and broken telling your dream to the same man or woman that has never accomplished theirs.

They walk away fine, happy, and go on about their day. What was this conversation for? What did you gain? How much did you lose?

Understand when there is time to have a conversation and when there is not. Like I said before My best friend tells me all the time that I have "Discernment of spirit".

It means to know when to speak and when not to, when to move and when not to, when to use these instructions, and when to use other instructions in this book that follows.

I have a friend named Doc and whether or not he knows it we are friends for multiple reasons, but one of the biggest reasons is that I see a lot of myself in him at times.

I remember having a conversation with Doc I said to him

"There's two types of people in this world, there's carry out people, and then there's Benihana's people."

Now if you don't know what Benihana's is, it's a restaurant where they cook the food right in front of you, fire, grill, the entire works. But for me, WriterBoy, I feel like the food tastes no different than the carryout's down the street, and that's where this analogy comes from.

I said to him,

"Benihana's food tastes the same way the carryout does. they just charge more and I'm not mad at them."

In life we all have the same amount of time, the same 24 hours in a day, and if I feel like my time is expensive and I want to be expensive then so be it. I'm no better than anyone, you're no better than anyone BUT if I want to charge more for my time than that's what I shall do.

I'm not going to spend my time arguing with a homeless lady on the street. My time is too expensive for that; Let a carryout guy do that; they don't charge as much for their time as I do, they're good, they have time to spare, I don't!"

I can't make this up ladies and gentlemen. The next day during our lunch break on production he went out and began arguing with a homeless lady outside of a Wendy's.

When he told me the story he said,

"Brandon all I heard was your voice in my head yelling Benihana's Benihana's Benhiana's."

I am pleased to report that Doc no longer eats at the carryout lol - hopefully; maybe, we'll see, he's working on himself just like we all are.

Moral of the story - don't be a carryout type of person. Value your time and what you spend it on. Everything does not call for a response nor does it call for a reaction.

Speak your mind yes but use one again discernment of spirit. Understand when the conversation is meaningless and when it really is time to speak.

//

Fame & Envy

So WriterBoy scored a deal with Netflix, amazing right. – Yes and no; you see with all of this accomplishment comes a lot more work, a lot more pressure, and a whole lot more eyes. As everyone watches the now 26-year-old WriterBoy become one of the youngest African American EP's to work with Netflix I see myself beginning to see myself, how God sees me.

Bold, Confident, Giving, Mature, Radical. From changing the lives of so many around me to speaking into people's lives all across the world I've learned to recognize the man God made me – and others are starting to see that too.

Sometimes fame and success can breed other famous and successful people, pushing them to reach new limits and new heights in the world. But, for those that sit around, listen, and do nothing but wish to do everything you are doing, it creates envious jealousy, and you have to be ready for that.

There's two things that I can tell you that will hopefully help you and prepare you for the battle of others' thoughts of you.

1. Know who you are.

What's helped me overcome a lot of the thoughts from the envious people around me is me knowing who I am. I understand the great man that I am and everything that I stated above, everything God made me, and although I am not perfect, I am the man that God says I am. So if you're describing another person, especially without even truly knowing who I am; I'm okay with that, because you don't know who I am, you don't know who God says I am, you don't know me - truly...

I think knowing who I am has also helped me cope with the fact that everyone will always have an opinion but their opinion doesn't matter - God does; and how could I ever let someone else's opinion override the opinion of God.

It doesn't, it will never, you were and always will be God's choice,

If God says that I am his, then I am his; if he says that I am beautiful then that's just what I am; if he tells me that I have an amazing heart - I'm sorry but I could never listen to anyone that tells me the opposite.

You're not him, your words are not his, and your heart is not his. What God says about you will always triumph over what this world has to say about you. - Remember that forever more.

So as I sit here I'm not going to tell you to hate on the haters. I'm not going to tell you to bash them, talk down upon them, fight them. You see because that's what the enemy wants - he wants chaos, temporal, he wants pain and misery, he wants to sow discord. - and me, WriterBoy, I will not be a part of any of that.

What I am telling you to do however is to one pray for them, because they see you how God will never. Two, don't challenge them, allow them to feel as you walk by faith. - Sometimes trying to change someone's opinion of you no longer becomes for them it becomes you wanting to change it for you. And once again THEIR OPINION DOESN'T OVERSEA GOD'S OPINION OF YOU!

Are you perfect? No, I'm pretty sure you're not! Are you trying? Of course you are - look at you, you're reading this book!

You may not be perfect, you might not always make the right decisions, but you are human, you're his human, his child - and if they can't see the strides you're taking, the sorry you offered, or the hugs you've given. You must know that their mind and their idea of you will never come before God.

And 2.

Forgiveness, just like with my family and the friends around me, I have to, I must forgive people for what they do not know. They don't know that they could have easily just asked for an opportunity, easily asked to work with me, to come aboard, to be a part of what I'm doing, it would be as easy as me saying "okay". Instead - they decide to throw stones at me to prove to the world that I don't exist.

Well this man of God does exist, he's here, he's strong, and he's not going anywhere anytime soon. So for those that want me to fall I'll pray for them, those that want me to scream, I'll speak peace into their life, and those that want me to change, I shall remain the same, and change their life for the better.

I'm not trying to be anybody else but who I am, and no Meir man will change that about me. I'm going to be and do everything you said I couldn't, everything you said I wouldn't; and not for you but for me.

I'm going to show you; I'm going to be living proof that No weapon formed against me shall prosper.

So yes, I won't scream back, yes, I will not swing back, yes I won't let it hurt me nor affect me and yes if it does I will forgive them for not knowing the man they were trying to break not knowing the future they were trying to destroy I'll forgive them for not understanding, not seeing, not hearing the God that I hear from - not seeing the God in me.

Because if you have to hate on another human being, if you must tear down or try destroy another mentality for you on benefit or self-worth, self-love, or respect you deserve every blessing/prayer that you can get, because you're not truly happy, and I feel sorry for you; but I cannot change who I am because you don't like it.

So yes I shall speak with all of my conviction, yes I shall pray with all of the love I have to give to everyone, and yes I'm going to continue helping and blessing all of those that stand around me. And yeah, no, I don't hate you – I feel sorry for you. Hopefully you'll see why one day and want to do something about that and change something within you - because of you.

But,

Until then let's pray for those that stand against us; don't lose your blessing trying to check someone that already lost theirs.

After reading all this, say amen, and then really live it.

BEING HAPPY

A little while ago I remember one of my friends asking me am I happy - and I paused then proceeded to answer him I said

"uh, yeah I'm happy"

It wasn't until after I got off the phone that I asked myself that question "Am I happy?" I then asked myself "Why did I pause?" I quickly got on the phone and called King Vader, again to you guys he's an amazing writer, director, and one of the most talented and hardworking actors in the industry - to me he's my brother. I called him and I asked,

"Hey Vader, are you happy?" he quickly replied

"Yeah of course"

I said to him "Let me call you back."

I hung up and called Eli Anderson, pop star, vocalist, and all around entertainer to most but to me a brother. - I asked him the same question "Are you happy?"

Immediately he replied "Yes, why you ask?"

I knew or felt like something was wrong with me instantly. - Because why am I hesitant to answer this question - what in my world gave me pause. - At this time in my life I had just signed my deal with Netflix, Amazon. I'm running an amazing and successful agency, and yet I'm sitting here pausing to wonder if I am happy or not.

I'm not going to lie, at first I began to buy everything I wanted, if I saw a bag I wanted or some shoes I wanted I just bought it. I felt like I have the money to take care of myself and make sure that I'm happy, why haven't I.

I felt like I wasn't happy because I wasn't taking care of myself but honestly I ended up realizing that wasn't the case. You see because after I bought all of that stuff and everything I wanted I got everything I wanted to do I did - and I still wasn't happy.

Me and God eventually, like always ended up having a long conversation, because I was confused. I remember God asking me

"What is it that you want?"

and I didn't know, I couldn't tell even you what I truly wanted and I told God just that, I said to him

"I don't know what I want, all I know is I want what you have for me."

God said to me,

"And that is enough."

I remember feeling this warmth over my heart. - Feeling my soul hot inside of me. I understood. You see, I truly do want all that God has for me.

It's not the car or the shoes, it's not the bags, or the clothes that I want… It's him. It's him that makes me happy, him that keeps me sane and whole, it's him that makes me who I am, who I want to be, who I'm striving to be.

So if you don't want God involved please don't ask me how to be happy because my answer will always and forevermore be him and only him. Money won't make you happy. AND TRUST ME I KNOW

HOW CLICHE that sounds but I'm telling you the truth.

I come from nothing, literally nothing. If you could see the place I lived before I became who I am then you'd understand me when I say that this world can make you happy, but temporary, in God I know I will always find more… and that's what I want. I want to become more, that right there is my happiness - more.

Now let's talk about you.

What truly makes you happy? What is it that you truly want?

And please don't say money, shoes, cars, and clothes because after you buy that first car 10 months down the road you're going to want another. After you buy that new bag 6 months down the line you'll need another.

This world is temporary. What do you really want, what do you really want to do, who do you really want to be before you leave this earth. Tell me what really will make you truly happy. - Write it down.

GIVE YOURSELF ROOM TO GROW

Give yourself room to grow, room to achieve, room to fall, room to fail. Allow yourself to feel. For so long I thought that my feelings were the problem, that my feelings were my enemy. But it's what I do with them that can cause the problem.

If I hit you right now you're mad at me, I apologize, you're a little less mad, I hit you in the back you're mad all over again, give you a hug and some money your back happy and okay.

I'm not saying not to be upset or mad or hurt, I'm saying not to allow your emotions to take you on a roller coaster ride. And yes you may fail with this sometimes, allow room for improvement - and Understand and be okay with not always being perfect.

I'm learning to be okay with that. God has put me in a life where I fight so hard for this "perfect" that I don't even see all that he has done for me.

I'm seeing it now, I'm seeing how everything I've ever fought for I got - and it's because of him that stands next to me. I'm going to always win;

the fight is fixed. So yes to my point again is it's okay not to be perfect, it's okay not to be everything … I may not be everything to me right now - but I know for a fact that I'm everything and more that God wants me to be.

Know that he loves you - know that he cares for you, know that if you were perfect there would be no need for him - it is him that brings you into perfection. So let's all say it together "I'm not perfect" no I need you to say it out loud. Let's try this again "I'm not perfect" - but I don't have to be, because it is he in me that brings me perfection."

Understand that you're on your journey, you're on your way to more and you will never stop growing! You will always continue to become - more. Get used to learning, used to falling, used to growing - understand that this is simply a part of life. I think when you do that, and understand that this part you don't have control in - this part is not about you - this is the part of life that you just walk through. - I think you'll find comfort in knowing sometimes it's not about what you nor what you do. - Sometimes things in life are just meant to be walked through.

FALLING

I said this in a interview with this amazing magazine/blog last week, I said:

"People look at me and just think that I have it all! They really think that everything is perfect and I've never fallen. That's a lie, I've always fallen - the difference between me and you are I've always gotten back up."

It's not that I never fell, it's that I never stopped getting up. I'm not losing this fight nor am I turning around - Which brings me to my point right now.

I'm in a space where I would rather not be - gaining more weight, eating worse than I have in the past years, and not really feeling in control of me and my body. - And there lies the problem.

Studies show that when your room is unclean, messed up, or all over the place 9 times out of 10 so is your mind - that right there, is me right now - my entire floor is a mess and so is my head, my eating habits, and all that I am.

I'm holding on to my grace of course, and listening to God continue to tell me to not stress or worry over anything because he has me but that's not the problem for me. - The problem right now for me is do I have me.

I'm sitting here looking around and asking myself why did I just eat 3 large fries and everything else I ate today? - Now to you that may not seem like a lot but to me … it served no purpose. - I did it because it was there. Hopefully there's people like me out there that understand doing things with no purpose can cause damage for a lot of things; speaking with no purpose can cause discord for a lot of things. I want to move and speak with intent.

I feel like I'm losing myself and on top of that I don't want to lose this body I so desperately worked hard for.

Which brings me to my point of all this.

Getting back up.

So although I feel like everything above and although yes it's going to be hard for me - tomorrow morning I will be getting up early, reading my bible like always, praying like always, and then getting up out of my bed, laying on my floor, and begin to workout (A FULL WORKOUT like I used to do lol) and push my body further than it has been going this past month in a half. It's going to be hard but I'm going to push through.

Sometimes when you fall off it's like going to the gym; you may use to be able to lift that 300 pounds but you haven't been lifting that for the last 2 or

3 months so you can't lift what you used to right now. You may have to start back at the 150-200 weights and work your way back up.

When we slide down this hill that we've been climbing up it's okay not to immediately be in the position you were months ago. Sometimes we have to walk back into our position - so that's what I'm doing, or at least I'm trying to do - I'm walking back.

What usually would have taken me 30-45 minutes might take me an hour or two tomorrows and I'm okay with that.

And If you don't want to walk up that hill again, I suggest you don't slide down it again. Don't take the steps back in your life, knowing where it will lead you. Like I have, trust me you're going to regret it - just keep your head forward and continue to look straight, look towards that future.

The quickest way to fall behind is to stop looking at what's in front of you and turn around to look at where you were.

Let me be clear, sliding down that hill even for just a moment is inevitable - we all fall short at times. I'm just saying these two things.

1. Do not stay there: The longer you stay the longer it's going to take you to get back to where you're going.

and

2. When on your way back up that hill do not beat yourself up if you can't do what you used to do immediately. It's going to take some time. Be okay with that.

I found myself today getting mad at my lack of discipline in areas that I've already got the training in; but I can hear my friends and family saying to me in my head right now "Brandon your human" and yes I know I am human, I know I'm not perfect - I just also know I want the best for me!

So yes I want to look good, I want to smell good, I want to feel good and all of this leans on me! It is all about what I want and I am in control of what I get. Honestly I just don't want to fall short - and if I do, I want to quickly get myself together and begin walking up that hill.

So I'm going to make a decision right now and if you're going through this you should too - let's make a pact to not get on ourselves too bad - just enough for us to get out of this bed in the morning - and get to work, and when I do fall, know that I am human.

HUMAN

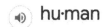 hu·man

/ˈ(h)yo͞omən/

adjective

relating to or characteristic of people or human beings.
"the human body"

Similar: (anthropoid) (⌄)

Human. I want to start by saying this. It's now 2021 and I haven't written in this book for almost a year. A lot of things have changed for me, a lot of challenges have come across me, and a lot of growth has been made. But the biggest obstacles that I've come across day in and day out and still something I am dealing with right now as we speak, very simple, Humans.

I find myself asking a question over and over again.

"Why are humans like this?"

At times we can be jealous, envious of others. At times we can wish upon others downfalls, look at other successes, watch others pain, and push for others to lose.

At times humans can argue about some of the dumbest things in the world, we can take everything and anything people say out of context, we can fuss and fight for things that won't even matter the day after tomorrow.

We can tell one another "I love you" and then turn right around and hurt the ones we love. We can say to one and other "I want you" but do everything in our power to push that person away.

Humans will look you in your face and say "trust me" and then you hear another lie from their voice right after.

This…. is human.

I think what bothers me the most is that I fight so hard not to be "human" I fight hard to be forgiving when other humans would never forgive, I fight hard to have empathy where other would not look to have empathy, I fight hard and try to have the courage, to have hope, and faith in others and with all that still they're human.

They lie, they steal, they cheat, they manipulate, and then smile, give you a hug, and tell you "I love you"

So you ask me what this chapter is about and it's very simple – this chapter is about humans; simple, but let me say also complex.

You see I've listed a lot of human flaws and I can keep going if I wanted to. Let's talk about how they have an opinion on everything and everyone else but their own lives, how they think that they know better for you (I'm one of those), How they choose to look past what they've done, who they've been, and see all the problems in the world but cannot recognize the problems in there self.

Sometimes I try to take a step back just for a moment and look for understanding of humans; but then I turn back around and rocks are being thrown at me by mere humans.

The same humans that I bless, the same humans I want to help. The same humans I want to love, the same humans that claim to love me. These humans are so confused, they're so hard; and I guess at this point I wonder why.

Why can't you just love me with all intentions, why can't you just respect me without looking for something in return; why do I have to leave for you want me, Why do I have to hurt for you to feel empathy. Why do I have to scream for you to see that I am here?

Let me tell you the harsh truth again, the reality of it all. Everyone will always fail you. There's not one person in your life (unless you die young of course) that will not fail you once or twice in your lifetime. I don't care if it's your mother, your father, sister, or brother and especially the ones you love.

They will always fail you.

Why? Because they are human.

And yes, it sucks I know. But people are human and we all make mistakes, we all make bad decisions, we all fall.

But here is my point.

As bad as I want to point the figure at humans I have to also point that same figure back to myself. Because you teach people how to treat you. You teach people what you willing tol take, what you will not take.

You teach people how to love you, and you teach people how to care for you. Now, humans are humans, yes lol. They're going to always make their own decisions. But if a person loves you, truly loves you. They will change if they see that what they're doing is hurting you.

But they must see it, they must hear it come from you, you must speak at these times.

I remember 3 years ago being on the bathroom floor crying as I started this book. For my entire lifetime I don't think I'll ever get away from humans. It's enviable that these cold, heartless, but loving creatures will forever be around. I wonder why 3 years later I'm still affected by them.

Of course not in the same way I've grown, I'm not the same boy on that bathroom floor nor will I be anytime soon. Even though 3 weeks ago I was but that's another story. I wonder why I still haven't learned my lesson about humans.

You know what I think it is. – I fall for their tricks; I want to believe that they are good so bad, that they do love me, I can trust them, they are here for me, they do have me. And so I do; and then they fail me again.

And now I'm stuck with the hurt, the shame, the pain, and all the energy that comes from getting stabbed and hurt by another human. And here they are standing in front of me saying "I'm sorry, I'm human."

If you've gotten this far and feel how I felt, I have an answer for this problem as well. But it only works if you're willing to hear me out.

Let me start by saying this first.

You're a good person, or at least you're trying to be. (You know you better than I do) If you're not trying to start, if you know that it is okay and that you do deserve more, you deserve better, you deserve better humans. (lol)

I had a conversation with God the other day about my concerns about his humans and how they treat me.

"You've made me this amazing man that shall take care of others, help others, change the lives of others, and push for others to become more than what they even dream of being.

I give love to your people, I help your people, I try to be the best man that I can for all of your people around me

Why do they throw stones at me, what more do I have to do? When are you going to step in and say enough is enough. When will you put it on their heart to stop it."

God was patient with me. You wanna know what he said.

"I never told you they would love, I said that I Love you."

"I never told you they would protect you, I said that I will protect you"

"I never told you to protect your heart, I said that I would protect it."

"I never told you to give all of you to them, I told you to give all of you to me."

Crying I write this because my God is so right. Sometimes I'm stupid, why, because I am human too. Sometimes I make foolish decisions, why because I am human too.

Everything I want from the world I gain in him and it's plain to see that he will never love me less, he will never hurt me, he will never give up on me, and he will never betray me.

It is he who puts me first, he who loves me the most, he who protects me, challenges me, holds me, loves me!

And that's why he's the answer.

For those that don't believe in God I want to start by saying to you that it's okay. It's okay to not understand, it's okay to be skeptical, it's okay to have fear, it's also okay to feel or be lost. It's okay to not know.

Not knowing, not understanding, not seeing, but believing … all that births is faith. - Blind faith. Believing in something you may not see just yet.

Now me being honest my God is way much more than just that and it would take me months if not years to explain to you the severity of me and God's relationship but I can sum up my entire relationship with God in one word "faith".

It is because of him that I am who I am, because of him that I walk how I walk, talk how I talk, listen how I listen, speak into people's lives the same way he does to me. People look at me like I'm just this amazing man - and yes I am all that and more lol. But I am all of that because of him, because of who he's made me, because of what he's made me; And it all started with me having faith.

You see God took me on a journey. - He touched me a long time ago and from then on I knew he was there, I knew he was watching, I knew he was listening, and I knew I wanted to please him, I knew I wanted to be everything he said I was. God's telling me to tell the truth so let me start by saying this.

I wasn't perfect, I never was; I also wasn't the guy you see today, the guy that's this "big" writer and director; the 26 years old man that's on Forbes. I was a young kid who grew up indifferent circumstances, in a completely different area where there was guns, violence, and drugs - and then there was me. My step-father sold drugs out of my house so no I wasn't a gang banger. I wasn't a thief, nor did I do or sell drugs; I just knew what that lifestyle was.

But also what I knew and who found me at that young age was God.

GOD

No definition needed.

I think I want to start this chapter by saying this. God is physically, mentally, and emotionally - my everything. It is because of him that I rise up in the morning, because of him that I stand up even when I've fallen.

It's him telling me "I have you" time and time again; it's him showing me that he "has me." time and time again. It's the fact that his love is everlasting; that fact that he wants nothing from me but to become everything he needs me to be; not for him - but for me.

His love is like a parent's love but so much more. Now let's be honest. Your mother or father may love you; I mean my mother loves me to death. But, If I shoot her in the foot today! She's going to love me a little bit less. Lol.

But with God, how my God is set up. It doesn't matter what I do, how I do it, when I do it - He's still going to love me; he's going to hold me, he's going to tell me that everything is going to be okay, he's going to stand me up, lay me down, fight for me, and protect me always.

Recently I just fell and his words to me were "Don't act like something's wrong when you know that everything is going to be okay." He then proceeded to tell me,

"Don't let the enemy trick you. this is my battle, not yours."

That hit so heavy with me being in a place where I'm going through a season making mistakes when I cannot, of falling short when I shouldn't. It is God that comes and says to me that it's not even your battle, it's mine - I got this.

It's knowing that I'm not alone, knowing that I will never be alone. It's knowing that he really does love me, it's knowing that he's done all this and given all this for me and wants nothing in return but to give me more.

I think with me if I had to describe God in just two words it would be:

"My Everything"

But I got a lot of pages to fill up so let me say it in a couple of more words lol. The following words are between me and you so don't tell anybody else - if they want to know let them read the book.

My journey with God hasn't been perfect, to be honest I don't think it will ever be. Now what it is, is amazing, breathtaking, and something so special. But perfect, it is not.

That's honestly because I'll never be perfect, and I don't think he wants me to, he's never asked for perfection, he's only asked for me.

The man that you see today was not the man you would have met when I was 15 or 16 years old. Yes, he was filming, yes he was writing, but the soul that I have now, the heart that I have now. I'm not going to lie and say I didn't have it then, I did - but it's something about when God touches you - that everything changes.

You stop to second guess yourself, you begin to know who you are, actually I think I'm wrong - I think everything changes because you begin to know who he is.

Before telling you the long and hard journey I went through with God I want to say this. - If you believe that God made us, if you believe that he made the trees on this planet, the animals on this earth, and the water that runs through our valley's you must truly believe that God is God - with that being said there is no cap on what God can do. - He is not human, he made humans, if God was human he would not be God. With that being said - its time for you to listen to my truth.

Hopefully you get something from it.

I had been filming for a long time, I think I was 13 years old when my mom brought me my first little blue camera. It was me writing since the age of 6 or 7 til that camera being placed in my hand that brought me to know somewhat of what I wanted to do in life.

When I was 17 a lot of things changed. I was gearing up to graduate high school, scared, nervous, and I really didn't know what the world had in store for me.

I remember thinking to myself: What am I going to do next, am I going to college, for what degree, what comes after that? I honestly didn't know anything - I didn't know what I wanted to do.

This recruitment for the US Army had come to our school and honestly pinched this grand life with no worries, many assets, and the ability to do whatever you wanted to do whenever you wanted to do it. They told me to take photography classes there and that they would pay for my college degree and everything. It sounded safe, it sounded guaranteed, it sounded like a future.

If I signed up they would pay for everything for me, take care of everything - I would be taken care of for life. They had me.

I remember contemplating on what that recruiter said to me for days, days that turned into 2 weeks, almost a month. I'm about to leave school now, I'm about to step into my future, maybe this could be my future.

I remember not the day, but the words so clearly. I was in the shower - I was thinking to myself - thinking long about what I wanted to do, about what I was going to do. Was I going to take this future that was being handed to me, Was I going to go to the Army, was I going to join them? I honestly can say I don't know what decision I was going to make standing there.

It was there for the first time I had ever heard God's voice.
He said to me:

"You don't have to do that. I have you."
His exact words.

I don't know how I knew it was him, but I knew it was him. The bible says that his sheep know his voice and all I can tell you is that when he spoke I knew his voice, I knew it was God speaking to me.

That same voice is the voice that has guided me all the way here, still guiding me today; that voice made me the man I am. So .... clearly I was right.

How do you know it's not just your voice Brandon? Trust and believe me. I don't always want to do what God tells me to do, I don't always wanna be how God tells me to be, nor do I always want to speak when God tells me to speak. I want you to know this lol. Even still I do what he says always, because he's gotten me this far, and what he's promised me is so much further. I trust my God, I believe in him, he is a part of me and I in him. I'll tell you more of why I know later. Let's finish this though.

I remember hoping out of the shower, throwing on my clothes, and running into my mother's room so fast, I remember waking her up and telling her

"God said I don't have to go to the army ma! God said he got me."

I must remind you - I was 17 years old. I remember her looking up at me smiling, no words, no motion - just this smile on her face.

I don't know what to tell you, or how to explain it but that moment was a moment I would never forget - that changed my life forever.

Now, I had never been the preacher's kid, or the kid that grew-up in church. yes, I went, yes I knew who God was. I just don't think I knew; he knew who I was.

But I tell you this, the moment that he spoke to me I remembered running to the church every single Sunday. Waking my mother up pushed her to go with me.

I remember being so corny as to wearing these Sunday suits and outfits every single Sunday. This little kid rushed into this building to hear this word.

At that time, I had just heard my God speak to me and felt like his words were inside of me. - I don't know; I think I just wanted to hear so much more! I wanted to hear him speak into my life more, I wanted to hear his sound even more; I wanted him.

What I found were people all in the same rooms wanting the same thing that I did, more of him.

Me and my mother moved probably 3 or 4 times after my first time hearing God's voice and it didn't matter where I'd go, who I'd be with, I couldn't resist running to him! I went from church after church still running and seeking his voice.

But not all was perfect.

Sometimes people get humans that go to church mistaken for God. Please don't confuse the two, because from a man that has been walking with God for over a decade now (and yes I know he's always been with me, that's not my point) from a person that has been running to God, sacrificing for God, and giving his all to God for as long as he can remember I know and I want you to know. Humans are not God; and please hear me when I say this to you!

They do not represent the love that he has, the grace that he shares, the moments that he will create with you, and the understanding that he shall give you.

Everything I'm teaching you in this book - I learned from him and that right there is the truth, it's fact. To my point - we are all human, but we are not God.

So say I love God, yes I hear God, yes I walk with God but I am not God. Do not judge him based on others actions even though they may use his name, even though they may stand in his house. This is not to say that they are a bad person, their evil, or they're the enemy - they're not, not at all - they are human.

Build your relationship with God for yourself. Yes, worship, yes listen, especially when trying to find his voice, but just know that we all have him in us, and yes sometimes he may and shall speak through others, know that we are human, human. - And if something doesn't fit right, if it doesn't feel right - know that sometimes there's God talking, and other times - there's human's talking.

God is someone that has always been there for me, someone that will always be there for me, he is the reason I am writing this book for you - the reason I'm here. He is my everything, he is my God.

Let me take this time out to re-introduce myself to you guys. My name is Brandon George Washington - God's son, his child, the young man he pointed at and chose and said you are going to be WriterBoy. Lol.

I can say it with a huge smile on my face and with all of the confidence in the world that I truly am his child and he loves me unconditionally. Me and God's journey started off so rocky. Lol

Well let me not say that. I'll say this - I started off rocky with God. Lol.

Growing up I was taught to stand on my own two feet, fend for myself, and take care of myself by my mother. She always wanted me to be independent and need no man for nothing.

Whereas God …. he wants me to do none of the above. He wants me to look for him, to need him, to lean on him, to learn from him. - He cannot work for me if I am doing the work myself.

Now before we get ahead of ourselves I know the saying "Faith without work is dead" but right now with God I've found out that there is order, there is timing, and you do not and shall not move until God tells you to move.

I was taught to be a leader, but it was God who taught me how to follow him.

GODS PRAYER

Prayer works, it works a lot. I can tell you one thing that's so dope and amazing about God and that is that he is always on your side. My God wants you to win, he wants you to achieve so many things in life - he has a purpose for you. And whether you know it or not he loves you.

With that being said he wants nothing in return but for you to love him back. I've never met someone like God and I know for a fact I never will.

When I pray to God I pray for strength, for guidance, for peace, for love. When I pray I cry out for help to him, I cry out in need of him. When I pray I honestly know one thing and that's that I want him.

Prayer does work, when I can't talk to anyone else I can talk to him. Sometimes I pray at the foot of my bed on my knees talking to my God; and other times I'm in a car, or an Uber, a bus, or plane I just simply talk to my God. No rules, no regulations, just my words to his sound, his words to my ears.

GODS TIMING

I know we've all heard the saying already, it's not on your time it's on God's time and I PROMISE YOU! IT REALLY IS!

See as humans what we don't understand, what I didn't understand is that if it came to me when I was begging for it - I wouldn't be ready.

You have to stop thinking of God as if you're waiting on him to bless you and understand that he is preparing you for the blessing he already has for you, he just needs you to be ready, to be prepared to handle it, and he's going to help you with it!

Yes - sometimes it takes time, it takes moments, and it takes hardship, but - it will happen. Your destiny is around the corner; you just have to walk into it.

One of the biggest examples that I can give you with God's timing is me knowing that I asked to be who I am today five years ago.

If I would have gotten it then, I would not be who I am now. I hope you understand that.

It took me growing into the person that I needed to be to even hold up this empire that God has given me. It took me going through the pains and downfalls of my life, the heartache and the depression to even know what it means to appreciate all that I have now.

Using the gym as an analogy - it's like going into the gym for the first day and lifting 160 pounds and your so excited that you did it you tell God

"Okay I'm ready for 660 pounds now"

It's not that you can't do it - you will - you're going to but right now you just lifted 160, let's move up maybe 40-50 pounds not a whole 500 pounds at once. I know your dreams are huge and I know you want them, you will get them but please hear me and understand me when I say let's just go one pound at a time.

Trust me I hear you right now saying "Brandon I don't want to wait, look I'm ready now! I can do it now!"

All I'm saying to you is wait until you get there ... and I promise you, you will be singing a different song! I promise you that!

I was yelling to God "I want it now" for so long that when the blessing finally happened, when the blessing finally arrived - I wasn't even ready.

You know why? Because I was too busy calling God telling him that I was ready and I hadn't even packed my bags. I wasn't prepared for what was coming, what he had for me - don't be me. It's coming, it's on its way - be patient and take it one pound at a time.

You see the things with us humans. - We don't understand. We don't understand anything; we don't understand everything. We guess, we pick, we choose, but to fully understand that God knows all, is all, and shall be all is something that I don't think humans will fully comprehend.

I don't know everything, but he does. I can't do everything, but he can. I will always fall, but he won't. I will always fail him, but he will never fail me. Can you get that?

To those that are saying this right now! "WriterBoy I already know this" or "my bags been packed". I have a few questions for you. - Where is God taking you? How long will it take to get there? How are you getting there? Where will you stay when you get to this location? What will you need? Who will you be with? What time will you be getting there? And If you don't have the answers to every single one of those questions when it comes to your destiny it's because you and I are not God. It's not our job to know - It's our job to follow him, have faith, and walk.

TIMES CHANGE GOD DOESN'T

This right here is something that I've learned over the years and want to pass on to all of you. Times change. So yes what was here today may be gone tomorrow. Yes, friendships past and even jobs and journeys fade away. Time may always change and tides may pass away; But what will never is the destiny that God has set in stone for you.

Yes, some things you've planned may not work out for whatever reason - times have changed. but what hasn't changed is your destiny - keep walking.

GODS LOVE

This is something that I've explained time and time again in this book but if you haven't gotten by now maybe I'm not the person to tell you, maybe it's something that you will get later. I might have been meant just to plant the seed in your heart for someone to come and water it later.

Knowing that I have someone that cares for me the way that God does is something so amazing. I just smiled and laughed a little while writing this because it's so crazy!

God is the one that will fight me for me. He knows more than I've ever known myself, he will protect me better than I ever could myself. And even when I make stupid decisions he will pick me up time and time again, no matter what. And it is because he loves me. It's not because of what I do for him, or how much I've sacrificed for him, how much I've given, or how much I shall give.

It's simply because he loves me. And that right these ladies and gentlemen is why I love God - so much.

He will never hurt me, he will never give up on me, he will never betray me, he will always be there for me.

When I fall he'll be there, when I fight he'll be there. When I win my first award he'll be there. When I take my first private jet he'll be there. When I win my first Oscar he'll be there, when I change the world in his name and mine - say it with me. "he'll be there"

My uncle, his name is Jeffery Washington; he's been through a lot of trials and tribulations in his life but just like me God found him at a young age, fighting to stay afloat and falling victim to this world at times; for some reason this man with God keeps standing back up.

For some reason God keeps standing him back up. I can see the love of God in my life, but to see his love in others is something you special, it's something more. I watch as God protects him, loves him, holds him, and stands with him even through his darkest times. God is right with him, telling him that everything will be okay.

No matter how many times we will fall, how much we go through, God will always be there. God will never give up on you, because he truly loves you. That's what love is, that who God is, no human could ever do what he does for you, love how he loves you. - He's something different, he sees something different.

I know that for the rest of my life no matter who may come and go that he'll be with me forever, life partners. And I know sometimes I'm stupid, I know sometimes I don't listen, I know sometimes I can be a big brat. - One thing I know though, is that no matter what I do, no matter what I say, no matter where I go - he will always love me.

That's God's love, that's who he is, that's who he's been to me, for me. He holds me when I've been beaten, rubs my back and baths me when I have been hurt. He fights for me when I can't fight for myself, and loves me even in my darkest hours.

God loves is everlasting, unconditional, & more than I could ever ask for; he is mine and I am his. And I love him for that, I promise I do.

GOD'S VOICE

I told you about the first time I heard God's voice in that shower but you should know by now that that wasn't the last time. He's been with me since the beginning of time and he'll be with me long after.

So instead of me talking about how much he talks to me, how about I tell you what you want to know. How do I hear God's voice? How do I know his voice?

Let's start with the first question that's easy. It's like I told you before, when he speaks you shall know his voice, when he hears you he shall answer. I used to ask why God doesn't just talk to people the way he talks to me, because so many people want to hear his voice. God says that everyone doesn't listen the same. So make sure when you do go on this journey to hear God's voice - you're listening.

Like I've said, first, make sure that you are here and ready to listen; after that - you chase after him. - Now yes sometimes like me he just spoke - but if you really want to get to know the God that I know, I promise you he's worth chasing after.

One of my friends a while ago said to me that he prayed to God and he didn't hear anything, he didn't hear from God.

THIS - is not what I'm talking about ladies and gentlemen. That is not searching, that is not chasing, that's praying - why not chase after the God you want to hear from? At the least you've done something more than sit and stare afterwards. Sometimes we must move.

I have another best friend whose name is Anthony Torres but I call him Glenn. Before meeting me, Glenn was on his own journey in life with God. He said to me that it had been a while since he heard God's voice and at that time in his life he really wanted to know- he needed to hear from God.

The world was telling him all that he was, and everything he was not - but what was God saying? I think that's what it was, he heard the world - but he wanted to know what God was saying about him.

Glenn told me he grew up Catholic so he first went to a Catholic church to hear God's voice - he heard nothing. Then he went to a Baptist church in search of God's voice. - he didn't hear him. He then began going from church to church; it didn't matter who, it didn't matter, when, it didn't matter how they praised them, who was passing him, none of it mattered to him - he just wanted to hear God's voice - no matter where it was.

It wasn't until one day he got home and opened up his prayer journal. For those that don't know, a prayer journal is just what it sounds like - a journal in which you write your prayers, your thoughts, your secrets, your conversations with God in. He opened that up and he began writing, he began writing all of the questions he had for God, all his concerns, all his doubts, all of his everything - everything he wanted to ask God.

He said by the time he finished writing all of his questions were answered.

This is what I call chasing after God's voice.

If you pray today or tomorrow to hear him more, YOU DO NOT STOP! If you go searching for voice, his sound next week or next month YOU DO NOT STOP! He speaks to people differently in different ways because maybe if he spoke to you the way he speaks to me - maybe you wouldn't hear him, maybe you wouldn't listen - maybe you would second guess him; maybe you would say

"Is it really God talking to me"

Maybe you wouldn't be open to hearing him. If you can though, I think you should - it's an amazing experience - knowing and hearing from God. It's something like no other.

And, if you hear from God himself, if you know his voice, no one and nothing can you tell you otherwise.

For those telling me, well how do you know? and my "I just do" isn't good enough for you. Let me tell you about some experiences that has kept me grounded in knowing that my God is real.

I remember being 19, maybe 20 years old and I had at the time three hundred dollars to my name - I was shooting a music video that next day in which I had to walk in there with around two thousand dollars. Yeah - we weren't looking too good.

I remember being so stressed out - not knowing what I was going to do and my friend Eli, the artist, he was so calm and cool - he just knew we were going to get through this.

I spent almost the whole three hundred dollars at Home Depot going to buy supplies for the huge stage that we needed built for the video shoot. Now I'm down to fifty dollars - one-thousand nine hundred and fifty dollars to get.

As we walked out of Home Depot and started walking towards the car I spotted a homeless man on the corner of the street. God spoke to me, he said

"Take all of the money out of your pocket and give it to that man."

I promise you I was looking up at God like - oh you crazy. No I didn't say it, but I definitely felt like it, and wanted to say that to him. - Now at the time I was new to walking with God. At the time, yes it had been a couple of years but I'm still growing, I was still new lol, I was still a baby in Christ - still am by the way.

I promise you - I walked right past that homeless man and straight to the U-Haul truck that carried the stage in it. As I was about to hop in the passenger seat Eli runs up to me and I lie to you not, he taps me and he says to me

"Brandon, give me all your money." I said to him "Why"

This man proceeds to say these exact words to me.

"God told me to take all of the money out of your pocket and give it to that homeless on the street,"

Ladies and gentlemen I dug in my pocket, shook my head, and took everything out of my pocket and gave it to this man.

Eli runs over to the homeless man and gives him all the money - he then runs back to the truck.

When he gets in he has this big grin on his face as I'm sitting there just shaking my head like we literally had nothing anymore. He begins driving with this big smile on his face and of course I ask

"Why are you smiling for" he replies,

"Because I know that God has us, it's not up to us anymore, he got us."

I smiled a little and then turned away looking out of the window. I'll say this - this wasn't the first time that God would have me give my all away nor would it be the last time.

A lot of times especially with me I have been so used to fighting battles by myself, I was so used to doing this by myself that God had to show me that I'm no longer by myself and not in the way of I'm going to handle the rest. - God would take it all away and then give me everything, anything I needed from him just so I could know it was him.

The key point in the story above was giving it up to him, I gave up all of my money, all of my fight, I relinquished so he can fight for me; I stopped having myself so he could have me - I stopped trying to get everything I needed - so he could get it for me.

Needless to say the next day when I showed up to set I had all the money I needed.

This is not an imaginary folk tale nor fictional Novel this is real, my real life. God surely does make sure I know it is him.

It was another time, I was shooting another Music Video of course and this time God had spoken to me before I even started to write it down. - He told me to write it all out and then find out exactly how much I needed.

I did that, and right after it was a little more than two-thousand dollars.

Immediately I was like okay bet - I began calling all of my clients; at the time I had run a branding and marketing company where I build websites, logos, anything and everything for businesses in the DMV.

I remember getting on the phone and making phone calls to all of my clients offering discounts for everything, knowing that someone was going to bite, and they did.

I got three-hundred sent to my PayPal in the first 30-40 minutes of me calling everyone and I was so excited like:

"Okay bet, three-hundred down - a little bit more to go. "

As soon as I got off the phone God said to me

"Now give it all away."

I was in shock - I promise you I was - How Could God tell me to give everything I own away. - That three hundred dollars was the only thing in my bank account and it wasn't even everything I needed. How could he tell me to empty it out? EVERYTHING!

I remember feeling so bad and asking God why, getting no answer in return.

That day I had to take my mother to the hospital and it was horrible. - I remember feeling so bad as I took the money out of the ATM before going to pick my mother up. I remember my mother looking at me so crazy as I told her that God told me to empty my bank account. I remember feeling scared and nervous.

We stopped by a Wendy's to get something to eat before going to the hospital because we knew we were going to be there all day. When I got out of the car to run in and get my mother something to eat at that time I had all the money in cash, in my wallet. I remember standing in line and this homeless person walks into the Wendy's -

When I tell yall he did not look to the right, he did not look to the left, he did not look at the menu, nor did he look at any of the employee's. This man walked into the Wendy's and looked directly into my eyes, and just stared at me; and look yall I was scared, I looked away quickly to that menu as if I was reading it.

I know we all know that feeling of someone staring at you - you can look out the corner of your eye and know and feel this person staring at you. Yall when I tell you - he was staring at me - like dead in my face. It was very awkward - and he didn't take his eyes off me. I was so nervous, scared, and confused. I knew what he was here for - but I just wasn't ready to give it up, I promise you guys I was scared. - So I didn't.

After staring at me for a little while he walked out of the Wendy's and I got up to the counter, ordered my food, and then grabbed it getting back into the car.

On the ride to the hospital I felt so bad. - I felt like what if that was the first time he had ever heard from God, what if he stops believing because of me. There was no if ands or buts about it - that man came in, looked at me, I did nothing, and he left.

Needless to say I felt bad.

When we got into the hospital I remember sitting down in the waiting room and as we waited for my mother to get seen. The ambulance had pulled up to the emergency doors and they pulled a homeless man on a stretcher.

I knew he was homeless by the clothes he was wearing. I remember how they were talking about him begging frozen because of the cold among other things being wrong with him.

I remember asking God,

"Can I give it to him?" God told me yes.

But, now there were like five to six police officers surrounding him. I was not about to go over there and hand this man money right in front of them.

No I wasn't, lol. So I waited.

We got called to the back and I remember sitting in my mother's room watching the homeless man in the corner by himself. - they wouldn't give him a room because he didn't have insurance, I wasn't thinking about that at the time, but how messed up is that?

I was still scared of course so no I didn't go up and give him the money then either. I don't know why I was so scared to let go, I think I was scared of not knowing what happens next, not knowing the possibility of me winning because of this. Not knowing if I was making the right decision. Remember I was still growing with God.

After a while they had moved him to another corner of the hospital and I didn't know where he was anymore. They wanted to keep my mother overnight so me and my step-father headed out to go home, I was going to come back in the morning and see her.

As me and my step-father walked out I remember walking past the front doors and there sat that same homeless man. He sat in a wheelchair staring outside of the glass windows in silence. I was so scared to give this to him yall. I want to be very clear, it wasn't the money I was scared to give up - it was the control, I was scared to give up the control of my life to God. I didn't know what he was going to do with it. I was scared to give it to him.

But I should have known like the first day he ever spoke to me - he has me, and he always will have me. - I was growing, guys, I was growing.

I walked past the homeless man and out the front door of the hospital. Walking to that car I remember my heart beating so fast and me feeling like I was doing the wrong thing. So …

I quickly said to my step-father, hold on and turned around. I ran as fast as I could back through those hospital doors and right up to that homeless man.

I remember saying to him,

"God told me to give this to you, can I give this to you?"

The homeless man didn't reply so I said it again.

"God told me to give this to you, can I give this to you?"

He didn't move nor did he speak. I placed the money in his lap and watched him pick it up. I then ran as fast as I could back to that car and when I tell you I felt so GOOD!

I felt like a weight was lifted off of my shoulders! I felt like I was free! At that moment I wasn't scared anymore I wasn't nervous nor afraid because I truly knew it wasn't up to me anymore. God had me, it was up to God.

I remember getting back into that car smiling with my big smile from ear to ear and my step-father asking me,

"What you smiling for?"

I told he what I just did and I remember him calling me stupid, and telling me you don't know what that man is going to do with that money, where is coming from, blah, blah, blah my step-father said a lot of stuff.

But you see how my God works - he taught me a long time ago before this situation that when I ask you to bless someone you bless someone - that's it. It doesn't matter what they do with your blessing, you've done what I've told you to do, you've blessed someone - and that is more than enough. So because I already knew that, nothing that he said really fazed me.

The next morning, I went into that hospital to visit my mother, and my grandmother was there with me. I remember the look on my mother's face that day, it was in disgust, my mother always loved me and supported me, but right then and there giving it all away she would always tell me

"God gave you five senses, you better use em"

but right now God was telling me to give it all away, and I'm going to listen to him. I have to.

My mother looked at me with those glaring eyes and she said to me

"Did you do it" I reluctantly said "Yes, I did it"

My mother grunted and my grandmother said

"What, what did you do?"

scared I told my grandmother.

"God told me to empty out my bank and give everything away."

my grandmother said to me "How much is it"

I said "three-hundred dollars" I then put my head down.

My grandmother looked at me hard and said "Come here"

I walked over to her scared and nervous for what she was about to say to me. I stood in front of her and she said

"Give me your hands."

I held my hands out and her hands grabbed them and she said

"Look at me."

"You did the right thing, God is going to give you that back tenfold, do you understand?"

I fought back my tears and shook my head as I said "Yes." She said to me,

"Don't you ever be afraid to do what God is calling you to do."

I'm Reminding you guys about one of the first passages that God had taught me and that was when Peter walked on water. God told me walking on water storms may come, he told me that the people in the boat my call me back, that they will be scared, or nervous, but it's because they won't see what I see, they don't see the god that I'm walking towards, the future that he has for me - the love that so desperately need in my life. - They don't see what I see, and I have to be okay with that.

And no I can't listen to them scream in fear of what may happen, no I cannot look at the storm that is to come my way. I have to keep my eyes on him - I have to, because if I take my eyes off of him I shall drown, and that's not what I want to do. I don't want to drown, I don't want him to see me drown. - In all honesty he won't let me. I'm smiling writing this because I know he'll save me just like Peter. But when he saved Peter he said to him:

"Ye with little faith"

Guys I don't want him to say that to me; lol. So I can't look away, I don't want to - I want him to make him proud of me, I want to make him happy, and I want to get to him, so badly. So I walk.

I love how my grandmother gave me that hope in the flesh to be fearless and to not care what people thought about me - to not become scared because of the screams from everyone else on that boat - because they are not, nor do they see what I see.

After that I was flooded with calls and clients one after another and had gotten more than three-thousand dollars in the next few days and I promise you I had never made that much money a day in my life. That wasn't normal.

I didn't understand then but I understand now why he did that. God told me to find out how much money I needed to get - he said write it down, find out. Never did he say now go get it.

My God wanted to prove a point to me, just like before, it is he that takes care of me, he that is in control, stop moving when I don't tell you to move, stop speaking when I don't tell you to speak, and listen to every single word that I say.

God said write down how much money I needed, he didn't say go get it. But I did, and he took it away, and then gave me more than I needed, in abundance. So mural of the story, stop trying to do everything yourself, stop moving so fast, slow down, pay attention, and listen.

So I actually have another story but this one is a little bit more complicated from the others, walking with God isn't always black and white - sometimes things get grey. Especially when you're like me and constantly try to do things yourself.

I was sitting in the car at a gas station of course with Eli because at the time he was my personal chauffeur lol. As Eli went in to pay the bill and pump the gas this homeless man walks up to me - he says

"Hey, do you wanna buy this speaker? I'm trying to sell it."

Now this was a nice Bluetooth speaker and I actually really wanted one so I was excited I said.

"Yeah, how much do you want for it!"

"Anything," he replied.

So I pulled out I believe like twenty or thirty dollars and gave it to him saying "here, here you go!" He said thank you and gave me the speaker and I was so excited. As I was about to hook it up to my phone he says to me

"Yeah I really liked it but I need the money so I gotta do this - you're going to like it though, I promise."

I stopped my excitement and smiled at him handing him his speaker back, I said to him

"Man I can't take this from you."

He asked me was I sure and I said "Yeah keep the money"

Quickly as he took the speaker back two little girls came from out of the seven eleven next door to the gas station and ran up to him yelling "daddy" and showing him the ice creams they got.

He smiled and began talking to them.

Eli finished pumping the gas and before he got in the homeless man looked at us and said,

"Could you guys take us to our house? It's really hot outside and me and my girls have been walking all day."

Of course me and Eli said yes and they hopped in. We drove them down the street to this run down motel and I got out with them. I remembered going up to the motel's front window and paying for another day or two for them to stay in their motel.

Mind you I am not the Brandon that you see and know today! I had nothing! I was living in a match box room with little to no money in my name, but I was willing to give it all away, always, because I didn't care. By then - I knew God had me, I knew he was always going to take care of me, and I knew I would always have him next to me. I didn't know about anybody else. I didn't know what type of relationship others had with him, so, if I know I'm going to be okay, if I know I'm taken care of - why not give to them - because I'm good, I don't know if they will be.

I remember leaving there and going straight to my match box room, grabbing one of the government phones that they had given to me, it had a certain amount of free minutes, talk and text a month. I grabbed that and put it in a bag; I grabbed a lot of clothes and shirts, and anything and everything I could think of, toys and all and we put them in a bag.

Me and Eli took it back to their motel and I remember carrying the bag upstairs to the man's room and when he opened the door to my surprise there was another person in his room. His wife.

She sat on the edge of her bed playing with her kids as he smiled thanking me for the clothes and everything. He then told me that she was pregnant and he had been trying to get his life together for a while now.

I left that hotel and told my mother about them and I remembered her grabbing as many clothes as she could, putting them all in a bag and telling me to give this to her. The next day I took the clothes back to them.

After that this guy would call me every once in a while if he needed something. - It became a thing.

He called to help pay his motel bill at times when they were about to kick them out, he called when he missed a job interview or two; called when he got fired from a job - one time he called for me to take him to the grocery store so that me Eli could teach how to shop for food the right way, spread his dollar. I was helping them, I was blessing them, it was good, until it was not good anymore.

So one day I got a call from this homeless man and he said his girlfriend was about to go into labor and asked if I could help take them to the hospital - I remember telling my mother and she looked at me like I was crazy. I told him he was going to have to call the ambulance lol. He did and it turned out that she wasn't going into labor at the time, but it was going to be soon.

He called back maybe three or four days later and asked me if I could move them into a better hotel, a hotel that was closer to the hospital so when she has her baby they could be closer to it.

I understood so I said yes.

When I hung up the phone God said to me "No" he told me not to do it. Immediately I was confused.

All this time God had been pushing me to give, pushing me to let go, pushing me to bless others and now he's telling me not to do it. AND YES BY THIS TIME I KNOW GOD'S VOICE! So why would he be telling me not to bless someone? I just didn't understand this question, and I was scared - I told them yes, and I was unsure of why my God would even say this.

So I left the house and picked them up. I took them to the hotel and they stayed in the car as I walked up to the front desk. For some reason the people said that I had to pay in cash and I remember walking up to that ATM feeling so horrible, feeling like I was about to do something that God did not want me to do.

So I stopped myself.

I turned around and walked back - I told the front desk I'm sorry and I don't need the room anymore. I walked out of the front doors and into the car and told them all that my card wouldn't work anymore. They were upset a little I guess; we took them back to their motel and he thanked us for everything.

What did I learn from this? Let me explain.

I was no longer a blessing to this family, I became a crutch to this family. If I wasn't there they would fall, If I wasn't there helping them would they ever get back up? - I wanted to do and be everything that God was for me … but I'm not God and he didn't call me to be God - he called me to be WriterBoy he called me to be his vessel, A vessel for his use and his use alone, not mine.

God never told me to bless them. I did that all alone, by myself; and my blessing became what I said before a crutch. I was trying to help and be like him so bad I felt myself standing in the way of God!

I cannot do that, I was standing in the way of what God wanted for him, what God had for him and his family, whether its trials and tribulations, or glory and justification. I shall not and will not stand in the way of God anymore, ever again.

I'm not him, I could never be him, nor do I want to. I was just a kid that saw how my God treated me and I wanted to treat everybody the same way. - And that's okay just as long as it doesn't interfere with what God has for them.

I don't know how to tell you how you will know but just know that he spoke to me and I may have felt bad, I may have been scared, but I'm going to do what my God tells me to do, even through my fear, even through my pain. I'm going to always listen and I will and I'm not going to step in his way; because he has work to do, and I'm not going to be one of the people blocking him from that.

Before all of these amazing journeys God took me through, it all started with me. It was before I made my first film. Now look I always was WriterBoy I always was destined to be the person, the man that i am today - but I wasn't always him.

I was not an overly giving person I'll say. Because I really didn't have it - but I'll that's no excuse or reason why because the moment i began to give it all I still didn't have it. There was no difference between me then and now nor any of those other instances. The only difference was what God had taught me.

The first time God told me to give money away was when I was 18 years old. I was on my way to my College. I got up that morning and walked to the train station. I think I had two or three dollars on me, I had two.

I remember thinking it was just enough for me to get there and back from school, but when I tapped my Smart Trip (metro fare card) I had already had money on it; I must have forgotten. Once I taped the card and saw I heard God's voice say

"Give those two dollars to the old man next to you"

Please remember guys this is before all of the above journeys lol, this was right when he had begun speaking into my life, this was after publishing my book and before making my first feature film ever.

When he told me that, I had this crazy look on my face like who are you telling me to give up these two dollars.

The comparisons to this guy in the metro station giving up two dollars to the kid in the hospital emptying out his bank account for God should tell you all that you need to know about my God and what he does to you.

Continuing on - this older gentleman walks up next to me and taps his Smart Trip on the machine and when I tell you this man begins to swipe his credit card adding money into his MetroCard; I remember thinking to God like "Oh God he got money." As he finished right after him another older man walks up and taps his card and it's 0 dollars and 0 cents on it, immediately he begins looking around.

I remember breathing deep in irritation because I knew he was the man God was talking about. So I didn't give both dollars I gave him one. lol PLEASE REMEMBER I was young, and this was my first getting started with hearing God, knowing God, and listening to every word that God says.

So I gave him the dollar and walked away and he said thank you.

I remember going tapping my card and entering the station as I'm going down the escalator God says to me

"Now go back up there and give him the other dollar."

I promise yall this little 18-year-old boy was talking to God like

"He's probably gone; he doesn't even need it."

When I got back up to the top of the escalator I could see him still standing by the machines asking around for money. I called him over to the gate because I could not exit out and he ran over and I gave him the other dollar. The man says,

"Thank you so much"

ungrateful I said "It's okay, God told me to give it to you."

As I turned around to go back down the escalators I was thinking in my head and talking to God saying

"He's probably going to go buy some cigarettes with that or some liquor, he probably didn't even need that."

Quickly God spoke said to me

"That does not matter, what matters is that you do what I say, you've blessed someone, that's it."

After that I had understanding, I understood what it meant to give and give freely. I also understood what it meant to listen. It doesn't matter what happens, when it happens, as long as I'm listening to him and following all of his instructions for me, all shall be well.

For people that don't have understanding of me nor what I am speaking of at the moment I'll take you back to a time in my life where the world was trying to make me question my God's voice.

I remember one specific day - it was with my younger cousin whose name is Avonte. I was at my mother and his mother's shop at the time. I remember the day like it was yesterday. I don't know what exactly we were talking about but I know back then after all that I told you I was going through with God. At that time, I was listening to God's voice. I knew who he was, and I knew his voice. I was radical. I spoke.

Meaning that no one or nothing could tell me that God was not speaking to me and when I made decisions or did what he told me to do I wasn't afraid to say he said it. I wasn't afraid to say

"God told me to do it"

That scared people, that made them think differently, they didn't understand me.

I remember my little cousin, a teenager at the time I had to be no more than twenty or twenty-one. He heard me talking about God to someone and what he had been directing me to do and I was excited to get ready to do it. I remember him pulling me to the side and saying to me

"Well God can't actually talk to you Brandon"

I remember saying to him "What?"

and he repeated himself

"God can't actually talk to you"

Now although I was radical and vocal about all that my God was doing for me I never forced nor told anyone that what they believed in was wrong, or what that they shouldn't be doing this, nor they shouldn't be doing that because I never felt like that was my place, because if it was, God would have told me. He didn't, so I never did. The reason I'm being open now is because he's allowed me the space to.

Back to it. - As I stood there he said it again.

"God can't really talk to you."

I took deep breath and smiled and said to him

"Vonte, do you believe that God exists?"

he did so he said "Yeah of course"

I said to him,

"Do you believe God made me and you?"

He said "come on Brandon yes of course."

I said,

"Do you believe that God made the birds in the sky, the leaves on the trees, the wind we breathe, the moon that shines, the universe that we're in, the ground that our feet walk on?"

he said "yes Brandon of course"

I smiled and said to him,

"So our God can do all of that, all of those things, can create all of those things, but he can't talk to you?"

He replied smiling saying,

"Ahhh - I see what you're doing!"

laughing and saying.

"I'm just asking a question." I then grabbed my bottle of water off the floor and the cap that laid next to it and said to him.

"God is like this bottle, open, possibilities endless
you can't put a cap on God."

So to all of those reading this that may not know nor may not have understood. - There is no cap on what God can do and will do for you - as long as you listen.

Almost 5 years later the same cousin Avonte calls me; since this time I had gone into the film Industry I believe shooting something big, it wasn't the Netflix show yet, it was something else; but I know I had been running for a long time in this industry as Avonte had been pushing on Social Media searching for more and making sure that the world saw his content.

He wasn't getting everything he wanted or the numbers he really wanted, but just like a true dreamer he was trying.

I remember this phone call because it was the day I knew that there was a light in me, and I may not always be able to see the tree grow in someone's life, but I can at least plant the seed.

Avonte called me, I answered

"Hello."

he said

"Hey Brandon I was calling to tell you that I talked to God today."

shocked I looked at my phone to make sure I was talking to the right person.

"You did?" I said smiling

He said,

"Yeah"

I asked him what did God say and he said to me

"It's not what he said it's more of what I said, I told God that I'm going to wait on him, I'm going to stop trying to do it all myself, it's going to be on his time, when he feels like I'm ready."

I remember smiling in that car so hard and almost tearing up, I said to him on the phone

"Avonte I'm so proud of you" and he said

"Thank you"

Once again this is going to sound like a fairytale but it is not! It's God!

The next day Avonte posted a new video and it began to go viral. All of the biggest blogs picking it up, from Worldstarhiphop and then on. - Everyone is talking about my cousin and he getting the views, followers, and numbers he wanted.

He called me so excited that day and I was so excited and happy for him! Smiling ear to ear on that phone I remember telling him "I am so proud of you!" I remember telling him now you keep doing that! You keep listening to him! You keep speaking to him! You keep running with him - the moment you give it up to God is the moment everything changes - it's not about you anymore, it's not about how you're going to make it, when you're going to make it! It's about being patient, kind, and giving all of you to him. I promise you just wait - watch what God will do with you.

As I end this book and also begin this new chapter in my life I want you to know something that I didn't know about me.

You're worth it.

You are worth the strain and the agony that you may go through on your journey in life, you're worth the strength that you will gain along your journey. You're worth the struggle, the pain, the decisions, the making sure that you are happy that you're not broken. You're worth it.

You're worth it, I promise you.

You should definitely know you're worth fighting for. I didn't know - and that's why it was a struggle for me to let people go, it was a struggle for me to treat myself right, it was a struggle for me - but know that although you're not perfect, you're worth it.

I think that's all that I have to say for right now, good luck, I love you, you got this.

Made in the USA
Columbia, SC
13 January 2023

10258044R00104